PENG
THE BL

Laurent Gally was the legal
newspaper *Libération* during
specialist in terrorist matters
Directe in particular. As an international journalist, Laurent
Gally has for many years worked for the *France Presse* agency,
notably in Paris, New York and Central America. He is an
accomplished sportsman and a collector of contemporary art.
Currently he is writing a book on international finance.

LAURENT GALLY

THE BLACK AGENT

TRAITOR TO AN UNJUST CAUSE

Translated by
VICTORIA REITER

PENGUIN BOOKS

PENGUIN BOOKS

Published by the Penguin Group
27 Wrights Lane, London W8 5TZ, England
Viking Penguin Inc., 40 West 23rd Street, New York, New York 10010, USA
Penguin Books Australia Ltd, Ringwood, Victoria, Australia
Penguin Books Canada Ltd, 2801 John Street, Markham, Ontario, Canada L3R 1B4
Penguin Books (NZ) Ltd, 182–190 Wairau Road, Auckland 10, New Zealand

Penguin Books Ltd, Registered Offices: Harmondsworth, Middlesex, England

First published in France, under the title *L'Agent noir: une taupe dans l'affaire Abdallah*,
by Editions Robert Laffont, SA 1987
This translation first published in Great Britain by André Deutsch 1988
Published in Penguin Books 1988

Printed and bound in Great Britain by
Cox & Wyman Ltd, Reading
Filmset in Baskerville

CONTENTS

INTRODUCTION

Fortunately, this book is not about today's events. The wave of terrorism in Europe seems to have retreated, a year after the tragic bombing campaign which covered the streets of Paris with blood during the autumn of 1986. Although this may well be just a brief respite, or one secured only by Western disengagement in Lebanon.

When this book was published in France, the media hailed it as the story of the year. But I would prefer English-speaking readers to find something of more timeless significance in my narrative. This tragic confrontation between a young man and the terrorist machine should not be read simply for its disclosures about such and such a terrorist network, or its speculations on the role of a country such as Syria. It also explores a series of moral choices, and subsequent attempts to act on them, which could devolve upon any citizen of the Western world.

Even so, the adventures of our hero make a remarkable story. The character of the lawyer-spy is by no means a literary commonplace, even if belonging to the secret service is still considered more honourable in Anglo-Saxon countries than it is in France. For, in the final analysis, the roles of lawyer and secret agent are the most paradoxical imaginable. The accused, whatever crimes society ascribes to him, has at least the right to the ethical support of his lawyer. Whilst the secret agent, beyond all ethical considerations, obeys orders out of a patriotism which can sometimes justify every moral transgression.

A psychoanalyst might be able to unravel Jean-Paul Mazurier's motives in attempting to reconcile such apparently contradictory positions. As far as we are concerned he is a typical Western man who, by chance, has found himself at a crossroads, faced with a terrible choice which could have a bearing on the course of our democracy. Should he do nothing, anonymously denounce the terrorist leader, or simply wash his hands of the consequences of the confidences he has heard? When interviewed on television the lawyer made it clear that, although some might have found the work he undertook dishonourable, he saw his decision as absolutely unavoidable.

Some people will be tempted to judge the man in terms of the effectiveness – viewed with hindsight – of his actions. However, the official facts are of little help as they are constantly being modified in a way which seems designed to confuse public opinion. The French courts have still not delivered their verdict on the responsibility for the bomb attacks, although Libya, Syria, and Iran have, in turn, been accused by the media. 'Terrorism is war', the authorities have trumpeted, and Jean-Paul Mazurier has certainly fought his own battle. Even if he is furious at having lost, he has never been tempted to overestimate his real influence, although strategists know to what extent victories in the field can depend on the speed of the liaison officers. In the end, one can only give all the facts, and refrain from judgement.

Laurent Gally, Paris, September 1987

GLOSSARY

Some of the political groups and other organizations mentioned in *The Black Agent* may be unfamiliar to non-French readers. Brief details of these are given below.

Action Directe
An extreme left-wing French revolutionary group, in existence from May 1979. Its activities became progressively more radical over the years, moving from symbolic attacks with no casualties to premeditated murders such as that of Georges Besse, head of Renault, at the end of 1986.

ASALA (*Armée Secrete Arménienne pour la Libération de l'Arménie*)
Secret Army for the Liberation of Armenia – an Armenian terrorist group which claimed responsibility for a number of attacks against French and Turkish targets in France, including the Orly Airport bomb attack of July 1983 in which eight people died.

CCC (*Cellules Combattantes Communistes*)
Communist Combatant Cells – an extreme left-wing Belgian group, led by the Belgian activist Pierre Carette, a client of Jean-Paul Mazurier's. The CCC, anarchist in tendency and anti-NATO, carried out a large number of attacks without causing any casualties.

CSPPA (*Comité de Solidarité avec les Prisonniers Politiques Arabes et du Proche Orient*)

Committee for Solidarity with Arab and Near-Eastern Political Prisoners – this group, which has never been identified as French, European or Lebanese, claimed responsibility for the series of bomb attacks which took place in France from the autumn of 1985 to September 1986. One of the CSPPA's major demands was the freedom of Georges Ibrahim Abdallah.

DGSE (*La Direction Générale de la Securité Extérieure*)
The French external intelligence agency, equivalent to the CIA and the General Directorate of External Security, also referred to as the *Piscine*, literally, the 'swimming pool'.

DST (*La Direction de la Securité du Territoire*)
The French internal intelligence agency, roughly equivalent to the FBI and the Directorate of Territorial Security.

FARL (*Factions Armées Révolutionnaires Libanaises*)
Lebanese Armed Revolutionary Faction – the Lebanese terrorist group led by Georges Ibrahim Abdallah.

NAPAP (*Noyaux Armées pour l'Autonomie Prolétarienne*)
Armed Cells for the People's Autonomy – an extreme left-wing group of Maoist persuasion, responsible for many terrorist attacks in France, none very serious, between 1978 and 1980. The political writer and activist Frédéric Oriach, one of Jean-Paul Mazurier's clients, was a member of this group.

|1| ALEX

In May 1982, Paris lawyer Jean-Paul Mazurier had his first visit from the man who called himself 'Alex'. 'Alex', who described himself as a 'militant Arab revolutionary', wanted to contact the imprisoned left-wing extremist Frédéric Oriach, a client of Mazurier's. He also wanted Mazurier to defend Mohand Hamami, an alleged terrorist recently arrested in Paris. During that meeting, Mazurier first heard the name 'FARL'. The acronym stood for the Factions Armées Révolutionnaires Libanaises *(Lebanese Armed Revolutionary Faction), an Arab terrorist group which had recently begun operating in Paris. Soon it would become clear that 'Alex' was a member of this group, if not one of its leaders.*

More meetings followed over the next two months. Before long Mazurier was to realize that 'Alex' wanted more from him than just his advice as a lawyer.

Jean-Paul Mazurier One night in May 1982, I answered a knock at my office door. The office was in the heart of the Latin Quarter, and I was sharing it with four other lawyers. It must have been after six in the evening because our secretaries had already left.

A bearded man was standing there. I remember his face clearly. Or rather I remember his gaze, which still sticks in my mind. The look in his eyes was soft but determined. He asked if Jean-Paul Mazurier was in. I answered that I was he, and invited him into my office. Once seated, the man asked worriedly: 'May I speak freely?'

11

Somewhat surprised, I reassured him that he might. He was dressed simply, wearing a suit, but watching him I was struck by the beard that half hid his face. It was so eyecatching that I could not concentrate on any other physical details. I cannot even remember the colour of his eyes, whether they were brown or hazel. His nose was somewhat aquiline, his lips slightly pinched, but on the whole it was a rather ordinary, oval, regular-featured face. I judged him to be around thirty-five.

'My name is Alex. I am a militant Arab revolutionary. I've come to see you because you are Frédéric Oriach's lawyer. I would like to contact him, and wonder if you could also take on the defence of another militant revolutionary, Mohand Hamami. I would also like to meet some of the comrades in Action Directe.'

Laurent Gally That was a fairly direct approach. Oriach, Hamami, Action Directe . . . so you were the lawyer representing suspected militants or people involved in terrorist activities?

J.P.M. Not at all. I was flabbergasted. Of course, I was Oriach's attorney. I'd met him through one of my other clients, a man serving a sentence for armed robbery who was in the same prison as Oriach. Oriach had heard of me there and asked me to see to his personal legal affairs: his divorce, that was all. I don't know how my visitor had learned about it; I didn't even ask. 'Alex' explained he was interested in Oriach because that 'militant revolutionary' supported the Palestinian cause, and the Lebanese Armed Revolutionary Faction, the FARL. I was unfamiliar with the acronym, and 'Alex' said no more about it. It is not in my nature to say much and in this case, whether out of laziness, or calculation on my part, I did not ask him for details but let him talk. I didn't even ask him who these FARL were and if he were a member.

L.G. But it was familiar territory?

J.P.M. I didn't know much about Frédéric Oriach except, naturally, that he was a political militant and had been jailed following an attempted 'action' carried out within his own movement, the NAPAP (Armed Cells for the People's Autonomy). Actually, I had come into contact with people involved in that case. One had left his identity card at the site of the attack, and

Oriach was wounded while handling the explosive device meant for their targeted victim. But in an attempt to gain time so as to understand the situation more clearly, I simply told my visitor that I could not reach Oriach for the moment.

As to his other questions, I was forced to make up my mind very quickly, almost instinctively. He was asking me to defend Mohand Hamami. As a defence counsel my job is to represent whoever asks me to do so. Therefore, on principle, I had no objections if Hamami, whom I did not know, named me his counsel. He and a young woman named Joëlle Aubron had been arrested in Paris in connection with a police raid on a weapons cache in the Rue du Borrego, and the media were depicting the two of them as being members of Action Directe. Again, I had only a vague knowledge of the affair and remember that after my visitor left I had to read the newspapers to have a better idea what it was all about. I learned, for example, that when the police raided the storage sheds being used as a garage at the Rue du Borrego, they confiscated a Sten machine-gun which, according to ballistics tests, had been used in an attack on an Israeli consular building. The FARL later claimed responsibility for that attack.*

L.G. Alex was not only interested in Hamami, but wanted to enter into contact with Action Directe?

J.P.M. Yes. I can't remember if at that time, May 1982, the alleged leaders of Action Directe were being sought by the police and if contact with them was illegal but, as a lawyer, I did not intend to become involved in that.

I was certainly intrigued when 'Alex' made his request. I had no links with Action Directe, whose demands I would read in the newspapers after every attack. But I did the same as any other reader or television viewer with no inside knowledge. Instinctively, I decided for myself that the group was doing whatever occurred to them, while making a big fuss about their revolutionary motives. In short, I did not take Action Directe seriously as a threat to our

* The machine-gun attack, on the building housing the Israeli purchasing office in the Boulevard Malesherbes, took place on 31 March 1982, see Appendix p.193.

democracy. At that time the group's attacks had caused only damage to property, and there had been no casualties. Which is why I merely advised 'Alex' not to enter into contact with them, telling him, naturally, that I did not know the leaders. Nor, visibly, did he, or I don't see why he would have asked for my help. Given my almost non-existent political background, I bluffed my way through the meeting, painting a rather emotive picture of the situation and saying, more or less, 'they're a bunch of idiots, not really serious'. I was feeling my way, wondering where this meeting might lead and what was behind his impromptu visit.

L.G. 'Alex' opened up to you very quickly after that meeting, didn't he? And what he wanted from you went far beyond simply conferring with a lawyer. Didn't that bother you?

J.P.M. Yes, but only during the actual course of the meeting. At first he spoke in a very normal manner about Hamami's defence. He did not explain his interest in the case other than as financial and intellectual support for someone who shared his own beliefs. According to him, I was to contact Hamami where he was being held in custody and give him a message telling him I had been sent by 'Georges'. I did not question that new identity. After all, he might have had two given names. Therefore, Hamami and 'Alex-Georges' had known each other for some time, but I still did not know under what circumstances. A few months later, reading the case files and the newspapers, I learned that Hamami had distributed leaflets claiming responsibility for, and explaining, the assassination of Yacov Barsimantov, the Israeli diplomat, a murder that had been claimed by the FARL. At the same time, in confidential leftist newsletters, Oriach was declaring his support for the machine-gun attack on the Israeli purchasing office also claimed by the FARL.

L.G. So there was that same alarm signal, the name FARL: a terrorist group that had already been particularly active in Paris, in the spring of 1982.

J.P.M. It meant absolutely nothing to me at the time. My political reading had been limited to the classics one needed for a law degree, like Plato, Aristotle, Saint Thomas Aquinas.

I had never belonged to a political group or party, nor even to a union. In fact I had only taken part – perhaps in a premonitory fashion – in a few protests organized by the support committee for Klaus Croissant, the West German lawyer who, at the time, was being threatened with extradition, and was being pilloried as 'the terrorists' lawyer'. My first real political act was to register to vote and to vote in the presidential elections of May 1981.

L.G. How did 'Alex' react when you side-stepped the issue?

J.P.M. He said nothing, and I don't know if he reached any conclusions about me. The conversation remained rather general; we were far from being conspirators. I told him what I thought, as if he had asked for advice instead of having demanded something specific. I agreed, conditionally, to take on Hamami's defence, dodged the problem of Oriach for whom I felt no particular sympathy, and pushed aside his request concerning Action Directe which, in any case, I would have been incapable of fulfilling. Professionally, and perhaps on a personal level, I said 'yes', but not politically.

Of course, it is easy to say now, in 1986, with four years' hindsight, that I could have, or should have asked 'Alex' to leave. But the truth is his sudden appearance on my doorstep intrigued me. Why me? What was behind it all? Would there be a follow-up, and of what sort? I was acting like a gambler: I wanted him to reveal more of himself. We agreed to meet again, ostensibly to work out the financial and practical details of Hamami's defence.

L.G. Did you have a reputation for representing leftist clients?

J.P.M. That's hard to say. I was very young, barely twenty-eight years old, but I was a criminal lawyer, a defence counsel who dealt with criminal cases in the Assize Court. In our profession that sort of practice is both a vocation, and a limited speciality. Among my clients were Philippe Maurice, the last man in France to be condemned to death before the abolition of the death penalty, his brother, Jean-Jacques, and others. I had also been named one of the defence counsels for a former lawyer, Brigitte Hemmerlin, who had been arrested for having attempted to help Philippe Maurice escape from jail. The court had objected to my presence, considering me too 'involved' in the case, even though I had clearly had nothing to do with it. Perhaps that contributed to establishing – at the Palais de Justice, and only there – my ultra left-wing reputation.

I had already described my total lack of familiarity with Marxist political theory, or even of a left-wing political education. My grandfather was a supporter of Marshal Pétain, my grandmother was a Gaullist, my mother was for Mitterrand, and my father voted for the French Communist Party. As a teenager I had come to the conclusion that that was enough of a mixture, and had decided that political party membership was more a matter of family differences than personal choice. And when 'Alex' talked about various aspects of politics, wandering off in a myriad of directions, I thought he must have taken me for Oriach's 'political' defender, not the lawyer responsible for sorting out his divorce settlement. Not wanting to undermine the beginnings of his trust in me I did not try to put him right, because I wanted to know where it would lead.

L.G. Did 'Alex' talk to you immediately about his political stance?

J.P.M. No, except in vague phrases such as 'I am a militant Arab revolutionary.' In fact, even though our first meeting may have had negative results for him, many others followed. 'Alex' got into the habit of coming to the office at any hour of the day or night, without making an appointment first, or even telephoning. If I was not in he would go away without leaving a message, perhaps for security reasons. My secretary would say: 'The Beard was asking for you.' Our official connection was to devise Hamami's defence, in which he was still a 'sleeping partner'.

We rarely talked about Action Directe, but over the two-month period during which he came to see me, 'Alex' made it clear he was trying to organize an 'internationalist' revolutionary movement. And I supposed that Oriach, Hamami, and the Action Directe militants were to serve as his auxiliary troops.

L.G. Why didn't you alert the authorities?

J.P.M. A lawyer is neither an informer nor a spy. We are told many secrets, in our offices. I did nothing, not out of respect for lawyer-client privilege, since 'Alex' was not my client, but because everything he was hinting at was hypothetical. I did not imagine, during our conversations, that I was moving towards a point when I would begin to take action.

L.G. Did you feel, then, a sort of fascination, either for his personality, or the theories he put forward, or his political commitment?

J.P.M. There was a kind of excitement each time I saw 'Alex', and listened to him. He was a change from my usual everyday clients with their often selfish, short-term interests. And he was elegant, intelligent, cultivated, the very image of a leader: calm, impenetrable, authoritative. He would never raise his voice, never become carried away. He must have told me he was from Lebanon, but he did not seem particularly affected by the Israeli invasion of his country, which was taking place at the time. He seemed to take only the long-term view.

Today I cannot reproduce the tenor of our conversations. It is as if I had attempted to erase them from my memory, and partially succeeded. Of course he spoke to me of the revolution, of the Palestinians, of the Arab cause, but on an extremely theoretical level, making no reference to his personal history. For example, he never mentioned Syria's role, Iranian fundamentalism, or Libya's international influence. I would listen to him without interrupting, punctuating his monologue with small gestures of understanding, barely nodding my head. I intended to convey that I was following his logic, although he may have believed I was showing unreserved approval.

That slow shift in meaning, that drift, occurred almost imperceptibly. 'Alex' was coming to see me at irregular intervals, sometimes twice a week, sometimes spacing his visits to my office ten days apart or more. But he was insinuating himself into my life to the point of attempting to make me go beyond the role of lawyer and become involved in militant activity. One evening he talked about his theory of the 'revolutionarily useful' discourse, in which he deemed it unnecessary to provide me with information which did not directly serve his cause. And so, not a word about his family, his private life, his personal tastes.

But he did have a specific objective. It was towards the end of June 1982, I believe, that he said, as if asking for a favour: 'It would be good if your office could serve as a meeting place for some of the comrades.' I immediately sidestepped the issue, falling back on practical considerations, stressing the fact that I did not work alone, that the other lawyers in the office would be surprised, or worried, and so on. He took it well, too well. He even congratulated me for not wanting to put the 'brothers' ' security at risk, but he never named those 'brothers', or introduced them to me. He must have taken comfort in the idea that, little by little, I was becoming someone he could possibly trust, and use.

From that moment on I thought of breaking with him, but could think of no way to do it smoothly. And when I saw him again a few days later Alex sprang the trap, handing me a letter written in Arabic, translating it aloud before leaving it with me. The letter was a text in which the FARL claimed reponsibility for a terrorist attack, the date and place having been left blank. I panicked, stammering something meaningless as I read it. 'We, the FARL,' it said, 'take responsibility for the attack committed on . . .' a blank space followed, 'against', and another blank space. Following that were the usual anti-imperialist and anti-Zionist political reflections motivating the attack. 'Alex' assured me I would have advance warning and asked me, when the time came, to fill in the blanks before handing out the letter to the press. I was in a state of collapse, but did not want to refuse for fear of reprisals, since I now knew too much. 'Alex' left without, I think, noticing how upset I was. I hurriedly burned the letter.

For several days after that I read the newspapers carefully, hoping no attack would be committed. Later, 'Alex' came to see me and broke the impasse by saying: 'Throw away that paper I gave you. You're a lawyer; it's not your role to claim responsibility for a bombing . . .' I was so relieved that I didn't say a word, much less admit the press release had been burned days earlier.

'Alex' left again without setting up another meeting, and that was my last contact with him. Later that summer, in July, if I remember correctly, I saw him again as I was leaving my office one day. Dressed casually, and carrying a back pack loaded to the brim, 'Alex' was waiting at a bus-stop. I walked towards him to say 'hello', but he pretended not to notice me and when I came near, motioned me away with an imperious wave of his hand. I obeyed him, and made no effort to understand what was going on.

L.G. What were your feelings a short while later, after the 22 August 1982 bomb attack on the Avenue de la Bourdonnais for which the FARL again claimed responsibility?

J.P.M. After the bomb was discovered, and two explosives experts died trying to disarm it, I was filled with rage and regret, telling myself that if I had remained in touch with 'Alex', progressively gained his trust and in that way learned of his group's plans, I might have been able to forestall the bombing. I still believed that I could have acted on my own somehow, without informing any government agency or the police. Not for an instant did I believe their claim of responsibility was untrue, and I imagined that from now on 'Alex' and the FARL would issue all such claims through their own channels. I did not think, even for one second, that this might be some bombing other than one I had been asked to claim, since it was the first bombing carried out by the FARL in the few weeks since I had seen 'Alex'. But at the same time I was relieved no longer to be in contact with him, and to be well out of a situation that had brought me too close to terrorism.

In any case, 'Alex' might return; we had not parted in anger. He had not even asked me to keep quiet about our conversations, as if it were obvious to him I wouldn't talk. In fact, however, I did not expect to see him again. Sickened by the bombing on the Avenue de la Bourdonnais, I had withdrawn from Hamami's defence the day before the trial was to open; in any case, the charges against him were dismissed. It was as if, out of spite at my own ineffectualness, I no longer wanted to have anything to do with that sort of militant.

L.G. Still, you had followed up the Hamami case and were therefore involved in the affair of the Rue du Borrego weapons cache during the preliminary investigation?

J.P.M. Yes. As 'Alex' had asked, I managed to send a message to Hamami in jail mentioning the name 'Georges'. It had an immediate effect and I promptly joined the other defence lawyers. Hamami did not seem to be very highly developed, intellectually, or even politically. I nicknamed him 'The Tract Distributor'. He had refused even to talk to the examining magistrate, but I advised him to start a discussion on Palestine and the Middle East in general with the judge, a favourite subject for all 'revolutionaries'. Ridiculous as it may seem, the tactic worked, especially since there was no solid evidence against him.

Hamami appeared very immature to me. He had been held in custody with another of my clients, an armed robber who had already been arrested and tried several times before. The two men had fought, Hamami had been hit on the head with a stool and childishly complained to the warden about it, as if expecting the other prisoner to be penalized, punished by being put in solitary confinement.

I don't think I was very happy with myself, but still, the day before the trial, I went to see Hamami. I explained that I had done my work but that the case no longer interested me, that I did not agree with his politics or his approach to defending himself, and that I would not plead his case, especially since he had other counsel.

During the preparation of that case there was a rather curious episode, which also happened to one of Hamami's lawyers a little while later. The front brakes on both our motorcycles failed while we were driving around town. My mechanic said it looked very much as if someone had tampered with them.

This incident, which occurred well before the trial, had no effect on me. At the time I did not know if Hamami would be freed, and did not attempt to renew relations with 'Alex' through Hamami once he was released. I lost sight of him – even though he was publicly alleged by press and police sources to have played a role in the machine-gun attack on Avenue Trudaine* – just as I had abandoned all contact with Oriach and, of course, with 'Alex'.

---

* Two policemen were killed in the shooting, which took place in the course of a night-time identity check on the Avenue Trudaine, Paris, on 31 May 1983. According to the investigation, several members of Action Directe were involved, including Régis Schleicher, who in April 1986 was condemned to life imprisonment for his part in the attack. Mohand Hamami, although also alleged to be involved, was never charged.

I saw no one after that until Oriach was arrested again towards the end of 1982. During his first appearance before the examining magistrate he named me as his defence counsel, but this time on the political side. Writing to me to announce the 'good news', he asked me to come and see him. I did nothing; I played dead and refused to defend him.

Some time later a group of people I didn't know came to my office, brought there by Régis Schleicher who was alleged to be one of the leaders of Action Directe, after Jean-Marc Rouillan and Nathalie Ménigon. I didn't know Schleicher, who had appeared, briefly, before the Paris Assizes for the murder of the two police officers in the Avenue Trudaine attack. He introduced himself arrogantly, rather as if he was announcing he was the Pope, and handed me a letter from Oriach. Not wanting to have anything more to do with those sort of people I had a fairly violent reaction and threw them out of the office. I was beginning to learn how to cope with terrorism.

|2| **A SPECTRE**

After the Avenue de la Bourdonnais bombing, Jean-Paul Mazurier heard nothing from 'Alex' for two years. Then, in July 1984, he telephoned Mazurier at his Paris office and asked to see him again. Mazurier agreed. The death of the two explosives experts had been on his conscience since 1982 and he welcomed the opportunity to learn more about 'Alex's' activities. Perhaps this time he would be able to do something to prevent further bloodshed. He realized, however, that he could not act alone, and decided to seek help from those who knew more about these matters than he did.

Jean-Paul Mazurier In July of 1984 I was recovering from a motorcycle accident at my parents' house in the country. At that time the news was not entirely centred on terrorism, although occasional stories were appearing in the press. Until they claimed credit for an assassination attempt on the American consul in Strasbourg, on 26 March 1984, the FARL had showed no signs of life since 1982. I still thought about 'Alex' from time to time. Meanwhile I was becoming bored, and in midweek I returned to Paris to check my office post. The telephone rang.

'Hello? *Maître* Mazurier? Can we still count on your help?'

I immediately recognized 'Alex's' voice. I agreed, and he said he would come to see me, then quickly hung up. At last contact had been re-established. It meant that something was brewing, that I might again be involved, even if only at arm's length, and that I would have to act.

Laurent Gally Your return to Paris seems almost like a premonition then.

J.P.M. The situation had been nagging at me for two years, and I had always regretted not being able to handle it better. This time I thought it through for an entire day, knowing that I was on my own and, from where I sat in my office, helpless to stave off any new terrorist attacks.

The next day I telephoned the Palais de Justice and asked to speak to an examining magistrate I had come to trust. I was able to reach his clerk, his assistant actually, who informed me that the judge was on holiday but that he could give him my message. I asked if the judge could kindly call me back, at my office, regarding a very important problem. A few hours later, the magistrate telephoned me.

'Thank you for calling, Your Honour,' I said. 'This is difficult to talk about over the telephone, but I have a feeling certain serious events are about to occur and that we might be able to prevent them. I don't know what to do, exactly. Perhaps someone should put me in contact with the authorities who handle this sort of matter.'

The magistrate made no comment on what I had said but simply assured me he would think it over, and call me back.

L.G. Is it common practice for a lawyer to confide in an examining magistrate in that manner, someone he never sees except during the course of a case?

J.P.M. The defence counsel is not the examining magistrate's enemy, and vice-versa, even if each has divergent and, on occasion, contradictory interests. That in no way precludes them having a mutual appreciation for, or an awareness of, the openness and fairness with which a case, or an examination, may be carried out. I had known the magistrate for some time, and knew he would do what was necessary. I did not have long to wait. Early the next morning he telephoned me at my home.

'Did I wake you?' he asked.

Actually, I had been unable to sleep, being too nervous about the step I had taken, which was causing me to break with my customary role as a lawyer.

'I've set up an appointment for you early this afternoon,' he said, 'with a colleague of Monsieur Joseph Franceschi, at the Security Ministry. Tell him your fears, and give him your information. That's the best I can do for you.'

That afternoon, at two, I was in the Rue de Saussaies office of one of the Security Minister's right-hand men. I did not tell him too much; I even avoided telling him about 'Alex' because, although I knew and admired the examining magistrate I had contacted, I was now dealing with a senior bureaucrat. He might have looked askance at the matter of the press release 'Alex' had entrusted to me, or even considered me at least a silent accomplice of a group that up until now had been operating with impunity. I presented myself primarily as an attorney for extremist militants, including Oriach and Hamami, and hinted, rather clumsily, at my desire to become involved in the prevention of terrorism. I even offered to resign from my law practice, as the word 'informer' horrified me. I had no intention of informing on anyone but, rather, of deterring the preparation of another attack.

L.G. The official must have been puzzled by, if not suspicious of, your unusual offer. Since you would not explain very much to him, could anything concrete have come from the meeting?

J.P.M. My confused story left him visibly sceptical. He must have taken me for a crank, although he assured me he would consider my proposition and come to a quick decision on it. Upset, I returned to my office. The next day newspaper headlines announced the dissolution of the Security Ministry as an autonomous government body! So I dropped the idea, not wanting to go back for a second try, this time at the Interior Ministry. Nothing happened following my meeting at the Rue de Saussaies except that two plainclothes policemen questioned my concierge, making the sort of personal investigation traditional for anyone applying for a government job. Considering what was at stake I found this approach laughable and gave up any idea of working with people who used such dated methods.

'Alex' did not appear again for several weeks. Unenthusiastically, I returned to my law practice. The telephone call I had been waiting for daily, and dreading, came on a Saturday morning in the middle of August.

'Hello, *Maître* Mazurier? Do you know who this is? It is urgent I see you. May I come this afternoon?'

I was forced to make up my mind in a flash. I was still on my own with no government contacts, but this time I had the feeling he was placing himself in my hands. I had thought about this moment for two years, but it was almost by instinct that I agreed to his suggestion.

L.G. Was this your gambler's instinct at work, raising the stakes on something you hadn't been able to control the first time around?

J.P.M. I wasn't going into it blindly. If I was agreeing to see him it was because I was determined not to let him get away again, even if it meant having to work on my own. I would have to regain his trust, even though I had no idea how to go about it, find out what he was cooking up, and perhaps manage to save some lives. I was still not the least bit attracted to terrorist theories, nor to revolutionary rhetoric.

'Alex' had not changed physically. He was still well-dressed, still had the same fire and ice in his eyes.

'How have you been all this time?' he asked. 'I need your help. A comrade was arrested ten days ago, in Italy. I would like you to go and see him, not as his defence counsel, it's too soon for that, but to give him a message. He doesn't speak either French or English, but I'd like you to reassure him. That's all.'

Once again I had landed in a situation I knew nothing about. What had happened in Italy? 'Alex' brought me up to date, in detail this time. Someone named el-Mansuri had been arrested carrying explosives on a train, near Trieste, and was being held there. 'Alex' called him a 'lion-cub', explaining that this was what young Palestinian fighters were called who did not yet have enough facial hair to grow a beard.

Seemingly more relaxed than during our first meetings, 'Alex' laughed several times while recounting the circumstances of the arrest. Mansuri had been travelling in a compartment on the Ljubljana-Paris express. A fellow passenger had tried to strike up a conversation and, when Mansuri remained cold and distant, for some reason took his attitude as a personal insult. The exchange became heated, and degenerated into a fight. At the time I didn't know Mansuri was only fifteen years old, but the other man was obviously stronger and tried to throw him, along with his luggage, out of the compartment. Seeing the scuffle, the guard inspected the two troublemakers' luggage and discovered seven one-kilogram blocks of explosive, each wrapped separately in a pair of trousers, that Mansuri was transporting. He was arrested.

L.G. That's not a bad story, but how did 'Alex' know about it?

J.P.M. I wondered about that, naturally, but didn't ask, remaining faithful to my technique of allowing him to volunteer information. Later, reading the case file, I learned that Mansuri was not travelling alone. He had stayed in a Yugoslav hotel – they found his registration card – and took the train along with Daher Ferial, a Lebanese woman who, according to investigators, also belonged to the FARL. So there I was, after that meeting with 'Alex', in the middle of a revolutionary group and entrusted with going to cheer up one of its members. According to police, Daher Ferial was probably in the compartment next to Mansuri's for security reasons. Seeing her comrade arrested, she took advantage of the stop in Rome to alert 'Alex'.

L.G. The whole scenario of the arrest is preposterous. Couldn't it have been the work of some intelligence agency?

J.P.M. Plausible, but impossible to verify. I later learned, through other case files, that Mossad, the Israeli intelligence service, had been on the FARL's tracks for years and might have been behind the arrest. But one cannot exclude the possibility it was all an accident, which is often the way complicated cases are solved, no matter what the police may claim afterwards. Evidently 'Alex' considered that the only possible explanation or he would not have been laughing so hard when he told me about it.

L.G. The fact that Mansuri was carrying seven kilograms of explosives contradicts the theory, often advanced by experts in the fight against terrorism, that weapons and explosives destined for use in future attacks may be transported 'officially', in diplomatic bags destined for the embassies of the various countries involved.

J.P.M. True, and as far as I know the members of the FARL undertook to transport the weapons they thought they might need themselves. 'Alex' told me the comrades even smuggled in weapons components, for rocket launchers in particular. Which does not necessarily contradict the theory of embassy complicity, but I have no way of knowing for certain. Mansuri was carrying Semtex explosives. This is a widely used explosive, made in Czechoslovakia, that has been found at the site of every bombing in France since 1981.

L.G. What mission did 'Alex' give you, then?

J.P.M. He ordered me to 'work out a way', which was one of his favourite phrases, to go to Trieste and contact Mansuri. He was cleverly making use of both my status as a lawyer, which would permit me to apply for a visitor's pass, and my supposed position as a militant. I was not taking on Mansuri's defence but merely bringing him a message of support from 'Alex' and, through him, from the rest of the group. We were to meet again so he might give me money for the trip and my stay in Trieste, as well as the message. But by that time I was trying to work out how to alert the authorities, whoever they might be.

Two or three days later, before I could find a solution to my problem, 'Alex' turned up again and gave me seven hundred dollars. He asked for a receipt, one of his own devising: I had to write the number 'seven' on a blank piece of paper, without even signing it! I had asked for ten thousand francs, which is approximately the price of an airline ticket to Trieste, expenses for a one-week stay, plus the professional fees a week away from Paris would cost me. But 'Alex' informed me that the 'comrades' had collectively taken a decision on what I was to be paid! He also gave me a small slip of paper with no more than four or five words written on it in Arabic, and instructed me how to show it to the 'lion cub' with certain hand gestures that would tell him I was there in my capacity as a 'brother'. Mansuri was to sign the slip of paper so 'Alex' would be sure I had carried out my assignment.

As soon as he left, I went to the Palais de Justice to see the examining magistrate who had helped me before, and told him the whole story, leaving nothing out.

'I'm only making this trip to Trieste to obtain some usable information,' I said. 'There is no question of my taking on el-Mansuri's defence, and of becoming the FARL's lawyer. If the authorities don't reach some decision about my future role in this business, with the mutual trust that implies, I shall remove myself from the situation upon my return.'

The magistrate still seemed sceptical. He took no notes but assured me he would consider the matter.

L.G. Did you have a clearer picture of your possible role in all this?

J.P.M. Not at all. I was going to Trieste almost at random. Having 'Alex's' paper in my wallet made me feel like a smuggler, as if I were transporting explosives. There was nothing special about the trip, except for a detour I made to Venice. It was the first time I had been there, and I was so overcome by its beauty that for a while I was able to forget my anxieties. In Trieste, I registered at a hotel in the centre of town, near the railway station, and close to the law courts. The next morning I went to meet the prosecutor and, in English, told him a moving little tale. I was a young French lawyer who had had a visit from some weeping parents who told me their son had been arrested in Trieste. They knew nothing of his alleged crime and begged me to do something, since they knew no one in Italy. And here I was, having come to learn what I could about the case.

The prosecutor gave me a visitor's pass that was good for one day, but I couldn't visit the prison that afternoon because it closed at two o'clock! Killing time until the next day, I noticed some strange-looking people at the pizzeria where I had gone to eat.

L.G. Were you under surveillance, or being followed?

J.P.M. It hadn't occurred to me at the time, but I *was* alerted to the possibility. It was not until the next day, when I left the prison, that I would be certain. My visit with Mansuri was short and when I came out again, lost in thought, I vaguely heard a motorcycle starting up. Automatically, I turned to look. The bike was bearing down on me and only turned aside at the last moment while I stood there, paralyzed. The passenger aimed a revolver at me, then the bike quickly disappeared. Of course it was only an attempt to intimidate me, since he did not fire, but at that moment I believed it was an assassination attempt. I was not being brave, I was being reckless, because I did not even consider dropping the whole business.

L.G. What about your meeting with Mansuri?

J.P.M. We met in a room inside the visitors' area; the guards did not keep us under surveillance. They had not searched me when I presented my visitor's pass, but merely asked if I were carrying a weapon. Seemingly happy to be able to practise his French, the guard showed me through the central control room from where they could watch all the corridors and entrances on video monitors, including the visitors' room. When the guard brought Mansuri in, I was surprised at how young he was. He was really just a kid, but his eyes held a wary expression. They had brought him from his cell, where they were keeping him in solitary confinement, deprived of all human contact, and I saw I would have to win his trust. Holding my hand against my chest, I discreetly gave him the V-for-victory sign; his face relaxed. We sat down. I didn't talk to him because he only understood Arabic. To distract the guard's attention I looked through my briefcase and pulled out a file, at the same time slipping the message into Mansuri's hand.

It seemed to me he read and reread those few words which linked him again to the outside world. Then he straightened, his face glowing as if God had personally sent him a sign. Using gestures, I made him understand he must sign the note. He scribbled 'Abdallah' in French. I read the word uncomprehending-ly. Since then, news reports have suggested that perhaps Mansuri was one of 'Alex-Georges' Ibrahim Abdallah's younger brothers, but at that time I didn't know the true identity of the man calling himself 'Alex', and thought Mansuri had signed his first name, since 'Abdallah' is a very common name in Arabic, something like 'Michel', or 'Jean' in French.

L.G. At that point, the name 'Abdallah' meant nothing to anyone?

J.P.M. Not to me, nor to anyone else except, possibly, certain intelligence services, including the one to which the men on the motorcycle belonged. I left after barely five minutes. Mansuri held out his hand and I took it, tapping his palm before gripping it with my fingers pointed upward, as if to show there was a link between us. It was both a salute and a gesture of brotherhood, of

29

complicity. In extremely basic Italian, Mansuri asked me to come back the next day, but I was unable to do so as my pass was only good for that one day. There was no way I could make him understand the situation and, my mission having been accomplished, I did not go back to see the Italian authorities.

As I was leaving I felt rather ashamed of myself, until the motorcycle incident occurred. Mansuri was a child and I had taken advantage of him, making him believe he had found a comrade, a friend, although I was no such thing. My airline ticket was for a fixed date and I could not afford to change it. I would have to waste three days in Trieste before being able to return to Paris. But since I had nothing specific to say to Mansuri, nor permission to visit him, and was worried about what the guards might have noticed on their video monitors, I had no wish to see him again.

L.G. The Italian magistrates must have expected Mansuri to name you as his defence counsel.

J.P.M. Probably, but I did not see them again. Which surprised the prosecutor in Trieste who claimed I had duped him, and officially notified his superiors about it when the full extent of the affair was revealed.

I didn't do much during those three days, but I could feel the atmosphere around me growing more oppressive. People seemed to be taking turns sitting near me each time I went into a cafe or restaurant. Most of them wore beards and khaki military parkas, which I thought strange given the heat in the city. One night I hired a taxi to go to a nightclub and the driver noticed we were being followed. I said nothing but asked him to return for me at midnight and take me back to my hotel. I spent the next two hours relaxing, not thinking about anything, but when the time came to leave there was no taxi. After waiting a few minutes, I saw what I took to be my taxi. It flashed its headlights, then drove straight at me! There again, my reactions were pure reflex; this time if I hadn't jumped back, I would have been hit. The air of Trieste was becoming decidedly unhealthy.

L.G. To whom do you attribute those attempts at intimidation?

J.P.M. To the Israeli intelligence service. 'Alex' had warned me

I might be in danger outside the country. According to him, I was not running much of a risk inside France, protected as I was by my status as a lawyer. 'Alex' knew Mossad was on his heels, and since he had been coming to see me at my office the Israelis must have wondered exactly what role I was playing.

I returned to Paris on a Sunday. While welcoming me back, my girlfriend told me what appointments were waiting for me, especially one with a man named David Besnard who wanted to see me immediately. I had other things on my mind and, even before seeing 'Alex', went to the Palais de Justice to describe my week in Italy to the examining magistrate who had become my confidant. He listened, not saying a word and still not taking any notes. I was a bit confused by his attitude: I felt as if I was holding a time bomb, but he seemed unmoved. No meeting had been arranged, and he had no suggestions as to what I might do. All that was left was to see 'Alex', at the day and time of his choosing, as usual.

Leaving the magistrate's office, I returned to my own to clear up my backlog of work. The only meeting I had scheduled was at six that evening, with Monsieur Besnard. He appeared on time. I led him into my office. '*Maître*,' he said, 'may we speak freely?'

I almost laughed, hearing the same phrase 'Alex' had used two years earlier. I had already sensed that this new client had not come to see me about a divorce, despite what he had said when making his appointment.

'Let's not beat around the bush,' he said. 'I represent the French intelligence services. We know you've just returned from Trieste, and who you met there. I could give you an hour-by-hour account of your stay. Do you want to collaborate with us?'

L.G. You must have been expecting it, after your meeting at the Security Ministry and your continuing reports to the examining magistrate?

J.P.M. To tell the truth, I had been desperately afraid I would not be contacted in time to help me handle whatever happened next. But now, suddenly, everything was completely out in the open. How much did this man know about my earlier attempts to contact the intelligence service? Everything, but I wouldn't learn that until much later. Monsieur Besnard was holding all the cards.

The word 'collaborate', with its unfortunate historical connotations, made me bristle. Yet, now that my waiting was over, I
almost wanted to throw my arms around him in relief. I plunged
right in and told him everything I knew, starting with 1982, not
bothering to put any of it in chronological, or even logical, order,
spewing it all out. He listened, took notes, asked questions, and
made an occasional comment. He seemed truly astonished: 'These
people have been operating freely, and we haven't been able to
take any counter-measures, or even find out who they are. Your
information sounds spot on. Finally, we have a lead.'

In the middle of our conversation the telephone rang. It was
'Alex'. 'Hello, when did you get back?' he said. 'Are you busy now?
May I call in?'

I hadn't expected him to contact me so quickly, since he had
telephoned me once at the hotel in Trieste, and already knew that
everything had gone well with 'the kid'. I was taken aback and
half-paralyzed with nerves.

'No, don't come up, I'm in a meeting and don't have time this
evening. Come tomorrow.'

I hung up, shaking. The two adversaries were confronting each
other right here in my office. This was a drama which could easily
become a tragedy.

Monsieur Besnard and I talked for about an hour before he left,
assuring me he would return the next morning, but not giving me a
number where I might reach him.

L.G. Did he make any promise?

J.P.M. No, and when I was alone again, and went over the
scene in my mind, I broke out in a cold sweat. I knew nothing
about the man; he was obviously using an alias even though he
now insisted his first name was 'Damien', which was probably an
alias too. I desperately needed advice and the next morning, after a
night spent in a state of total panic, I went to the office of the
magistrate who had become my mentor. He greeted me icily.

'You're incredibly reckless,' he said. 'How do you know the man
wasn't a member of FARL, one of "Alex's" comrades sent to test
you? And what if you've been "burned"? You may have fallen into
a crude trap. If you see the man today, ask him to prove he belongs
to the DGSE.'

More nervous than ever, I went back to my office and downed a full bottle of whisky, but even that didn't help and I ended up moaning to my secretary: 'They're going to kill me, they're going to kill me . . .'

Luckily, despite our plans to meet, 'Alex' did not appear. I was almost delirious with drink and anxiety. Monsieur Besnard called that evening and asked me to meet him at a cafe. When we met, I told him about my morning visit to the magistrate and then, like a contrary child, I shut up. Besnard tried to allay my fears, tried to convince me of his identity, but there was no way he could prove he was working for the *Piscine*. Naturally, they don't pass out identification cards, or badges. Having told him all I knew, I was now completely in his hands, forced to trust him since I could no longer turn back. Nothing constructive came of that meeting, and we agreed to see each other again the next day.

But it was 'Alex' I saw first. He was in a good mood when he arrived at my office, seemingly proud of his new militant lawyer. Scrutinizing Mansuri's signature he seemed surprised at the word 'Abdallah'. He made me go over the high points of my trip. I told him of the 'incidents' with the motorcycle and the taxi, which he found funny. Then, becoming serious, he changed the subject.

'You know, you must go and see Oriach in prison,' he said. 'My comrades and I are considering the possibility of a widespread operation the like of which has never been seen, at least in the West. Something similar was carried out successfully once before, elsewhere. We'll use it to free "the kid" and Oriach, and other comrades as well.' He began listing names which meant nothing to me: Italian, German, and the Japanese who was in prison in Israel for the Lod Airport massacre.

'We already know not all the countries involved will accede to our demands, but we will refuse any compromise, or any partial satisfaction of our aims. All the comrades must be freed, and if the countries refuse we have programmed a second, even more decisive, operation.'

This information was of considerable importance, and I dared not risk asking him for details. I knew Oriach had been sent to prison for five years for what was to all intents and purposes the crime of having the wrong political opinions. He had openly approved several attacks for which Action Directe claimed responsibility, and had already publicly supported the FARL in 1982.

L.G. Each new stage of the affair seemed to occur when either you or 'Alex' (if not 'Damien', who scarcely knew you) suddenly disclosed something. Were you being naive?

J.P.M. Neither 'Alex', nor 'Damien', nor I had any choice. I believe that at that time the *Piscine* regarded me as an unexpected means of infiltrating the FARL. Even though, in 1982, I had not openly displayed my reservations regarding 'Alex', he had dropped me. If he was turning to me now it was no doubt because I was the one person who could get in to see Mansuri. As for me, I was in an awkward situation, and the rash acts I committed were in direct proportion to the difficulties of my position and my feelings of anxiety at being totally on my own.

|3| **THE RECRUIT**

Once he had made contact with the DGSE, Mazurier was soon initiated into the world of the secret service. He was assigned a handler named 'Antoine' and himself adopted the code name 'Simon'. He had become a 'Black Agent', working almost full-time for the service under cover of his profession.

Meanwhile, 'Alex' continued to be a regular visitor to his office, and soon Mazurier was able to pass some vital information on to his masters – the date of the FARL's planned 'operation'.

Jean-Paul Mazurier 'Alex' described that planned operation early in the evening. He hadn't been gone an hour when 'Damien' was seated in the same armchair. I was incredibly excited, but nervous. 'Alex' had led me to believe that at each of his visits several 'comrades' kept the area around my office under surveillance to make sure the coast was clear. I think that surveillance team left when 'Alex' did. And as for the Service's own security measures, 'Damien' told me that since the *Piscine* knew almost nothing about the FARL, they would not immediately place my building under surveillance to avoid attracting their attention.

All I really wanted was to receive some assurances. This was our third meeting and 'Damien' admitted, somewhat confusedly, that he had been reprimanded for not having managed to win my trust. He then invited me to meet some of his superior officers at a police barracks, to authenticate the fact that he was acting officially.

Laurent Gally 'Damien' could have been working for the DST, the counter-intelligence agency that operates inside France!

J.P.M. Yes. I refused his offer, convinced that it was legitimate but not wanting actually to go through with it. 'Damien' gave me the telephone number of the *Piscine*'s switchboard, which is classified, as well as his own extension number. After he left I quickly dialled the number and was taken aback when I was put on 'hold', with some music designed to keep me waiting patiently, the first few bars of an old Nino Ferrer song, *Le Sud*, with its supposedly soothing lyrics.

Once I was satisfied as to 'Damien's' *bona fides*, I reported on 'Alex's' most recent plans. I made it clear that, according to 'Alex', the operation being planned was targeted primarily at French interests so as to justify the demands for Frédéric Oriach's release, but that it would not take place inside France. We wasted a lot of time trying to guess what form the operation might take: an aeroplane hijacking, or a suicide-squad attack against the UN forces in Lebanon, taking hostage diplomats from one or more of the countries involved. Obviously, we had no way of knowing.

Rather than waste more time inventing scenarios, 'Damien' preferred to report quickly to his superiors about 'Alex's' plans. It was obvious he believed what I was saying, even if the scope of the planned attack left him somewhat bemused.

L.G. So, no sooner did the DGSE actually contact you, than you handed them this new information on a plate. Didn't it seem too good to be true?

J.P.M. That's possible, but 'they' couldn't ignore information of such importance. Of course, I didn't immediately trust the Service, and vice-versa. In fact, quite the opposite: for more than six months I had the impression they were still suspicious of me. At almost every meeting my handler would say: 'But why did all these revolutionaries decide to trust you? It can't be merely for professional reasons! You haven't just been representing them. You must have been helping them in some concrete manner. You can tell us. We'll wipe the slate clean if you're the one who claimed responsibility for the Avenue de la Bourdonnais attack. What's past is past.'

I had to prove my good faith by attempting to learn how the

press release claiming responsibility for that attack had been produced in Greece, or Beirut. I could understand the Service's position even though I didn't agree with it. After all, I was in an even more difficult situation, constantly being forced to prove my good faith to both sides.

L.G. Did you see anyone, besides 'Damien'?

J.P.M. He disappeared after three weeks, passing me on to 'Antoine', as if he were incapable of handling the affair, given its growing complexity. Actually, there had been no real empathy between 'Damien' and me, although I immediately felt comfortable with 'Antoine'. He was the only one I would ever see, except when he was away on an assignment and 'Christian' took over. I have no hesitation about using those names since they were aliases the men were using in their work. I chose a code name to use when telephoning the Service: I opted for 'Simon', from one of my favourite songs.

L.G. Isn't there something 'knightly' about joining the *Piscine*?

J.P.M. Why not? It's all rather Faustian, really: you enter the Service, but you may never leave it. The Service may leave you, or put you on ice for an indeterminate length of time, and then call you back to active service whenever it chooses. 'Damien' explained the rules to me during our first meetings. But in the meantime, I was obsessed only by the practical problem of deterring the attack, insofar as 'Alex' might give me the opportunity to do so.

The Service wanted me to 'work out a way' – their style of language was much the same as 'Alex's' – to learn as many details as I could about the operation. The next time I saw 'Alex' he mentioned something about October 15th, but perhaps he was trying to calm me down, and put an end to the pointed, somewhat awkward, questions I was asking.

'I must be ready when the time comes,' I told him. 'I don't want to be in the middle of an important case. I don't want to know how and where it will happen, but I do have to know when it will happen, so I can make myself available.'

My reasoning was good, but undoubtedly I must have seemed anxious. Even though I didn't know if the date corresponded with some past historical event in Middle-Eastern, or Palestinian history, I was taking it seriously. The Service was also readying itself for the day, putting itself on a war footing. It was now the end of September, or the beginning of October, 1984.

L.G. Did 'Alex' have any particular assignment in mind for you during that operation?

J.P.M. No, and he was becoming more and more careful. We were no longer meeting at my office. After each telephone call I would have to meet him at a phone box, arriving precisely five minutes after he hung up. Following a predetermined route, I would walk fifty yards behind him to where we would meet, in a cafe near my office. These precautions seemed ridiculous to me.

Although 'Alex' was no longer talking about the October 15th operation, he did bring me in on another project being organized for the beginning of October. His group, he told me, had 'strategic material' – weapons – at one of its hideouts. He wanted to put what he called 'these very sophisticated weapons', which supposedly could all fit into one suitcase, in a safe place. 'Alex' was quite explicit that the weapons he was talking about were not meant to be used in the October 15th operation but in the next one, which would be a follow-up to the first in case it failed. But he was betting there would be so much 'repression', that is, so much police activity, after October 15th that he wanted to hide the weapons.

L.G. Was he making you responsible for those weapons?

J.P.M. Yes, and that surprised me, but he didn't say so directly. Before mentioning the existence of that small arsenal 'Alex' studied me carefully, then said: 'My comrades and I have realized we know nothing about you. We've talked together several times, but I know nothing about your life. Tell me about yourself.'

I felt as if I were facing a lie-detector. I realized this was an important moment and tried to reassure him by first reminding him how I had made myself 'available' in 1982, and how I had kept silent since. Then I spoke to him of my family, trying to make it sound perfectly ordinary, and about my equally normal personal life, and about my work. I expressed criticism of my profession for its social conservatism and formalism, and assured him, in turn, that I felt he was making it possible for me to become 'revolutionarily useful'. I cited Oriach, Hamami, the trip to Trieste: in brief, all the missions 'Alex' had given me and that I had carried out.

Looking back now, I think he was not so much trying to trap me as to reassure himself as to the original favourable opinion he had had of me. After all, a new wave of activist lawyers had appeared at the Palais de Justice since 1982, but he had come back to see me. Over the next three hours I recited the entire catalogue of revolutionary theory and answered all 'Alex's' questions with what his phrasing of them suggested were the correct answers.

L.G. Listening to you, one might doubt 'Alex's' IQ.

J.P.M. No, he was of superior intelligence, but he was already half-convinced. Suspecting me now would have obliged him to question his own judgement, and he would have had to start all over again from the beginning, establishing new contacts, with no guarantee of success. He knew I hadn't talked. Strangely enough, any doubts he had were that he might not be my only revolutionary mentor, and that I might use the weapons he was going to entrust to me for other operations by other militants I might know. It may seem strange, but in those circles as much time is spent suspecting each other as suspecting the outside world. I would later discover that the same attitude also existed inside the DGSE.

Once 'Alex' was reassured, we made plans to hide the weapons. I had no car. His plans called for two. He and I would lead the way in one; the other would carry the 'comrades' and the 'strategic material'. We would keep in touch by walkie-talkie. My task was to find a new hiding place for the weapons, and then to keep an eye on them. 'Alex' did not reveal his group's hideouts to me, but he did tell me there were several, of two different sorts: temporary hiding places which they changed every two or three months, and permanent hideouts that could be left as 'sleepers' for years. If this was true, 'Alex's' logistics were very well organized.

L.G. That doesn't match up with his giving you responsibility for the weapons cache. Why couldn't the group move the weapons to one of their permanent hideouts without your help?

J.P.M. You must not forget the operation that had been set for October 15th. 'Alex' and his comrades would be taking part in it, outside France. He must have been planning for me to deliver the weapons in time for the second phase of the operation. Perhaps

'Alex' was also afraid of police searches, since no hideout is ever totally secure. But I was a lawyer, although not the FARL's lawyer since I was not representing Mansuri, and would have no problems transporting a suitcase wherever they might want me to bring it, after I had dug up the weapons. 'Alex' probably based this on his memories of the 'baggage carriers' who operated during the Algerian War.

Together, we decided to bury the suitcase of weapons . . . in the garden of my parents' house in the country. Which should have convinced him how little I had to offer, logistically. What appeared to bother him most was that I had no access to a car. Still, we established a schedule and an itinerary. I was to remain available on the next, and the following, weekend and 'Alex' would come for me at my office. This led me to suppose that his weapons cache was in Paris, although I had no more specific details.

Totally exhausted, I left him at around ten that evening and immediately telephoned the *Piscine* to inform my contact of this new turn of events. A meeting was arranged for early the next morning. At that time I was still seeing 'Damien'; I gave him as detailed a report as I could of the previous night's meeting. He was to report to his superiors, and we were to meet again later.

As usual, 'they' ordered me to do whatever 'Alex' wanted. He was asking me to 'manage' to find a car somehow, but I was sticking to my claim of poverty, as the Service wanted me to 'manage' to convince him I couldn't. 'They' wanted 'Alex' to be forced into renting a car and paying for it at the rental agency with a credit card which would reveal his identity. As for the weapons cache, 'Damien' promised me the Service would not interfere, would keep both the road clear and the cars under surveillance.

I was feeling awful. How could 'Alex' actually believe I didn't have even one friend who might lend me his car for the day, nor a credit card to rent one? As for the DGSE, I felt no confidence in them either. What if, at some point during the four-hundred-kilometre odyssey, they stopped the convoy? What a feather in the Service's cap! And what a windfall for the media! I couldn't believe they would only hold me in custody for forty-eight hours, then calmly allow me to return to my law practice.

When I expressed my fears to 'Damien' he awkwardly attempted to reassure me, saying that forty-eight hours in police custody wasn't that unbearable an ordeal! But I wanted 'them' to absolve me of all responsibility, and make certain 'Alex' would never suspect a thing. The *Piscine* had taken to referring to the plan as 'Operation Gardening', and it was beginning to look as if it might turn into a disaster for me. Obviously, 'Alex' and his friends would be armed and would never allow themselves to be arrested quietly. I did not want to be caught in the crossfire.

L.G. At this point, were you officially a paid agent of the Service?

J.P.M. Yes, but there was no proof that I was. I'm not a member of the military like Commandant Mafart, or Captain Prieur, the agents who were caught red-handed in New Zealand during the *Rainbow Warrior* affair and were able to identify themselves as French officers. There was no question of my protesting my innocence to the gendarmes and insisting that I was acting on the Service's orders. The Service would have had no problem denying it. As for the money, the pay was ridiculous – about two thousand francs a month at the start – but I wasn't doing it for the money.

If I was going to fight terrorism, I had no intention of allowing myself to be classified in the same category as the terrorists, despite appearances. 'Damien' could not give me any assurances about that, which was, I imagine, what led to him being replaced by 'Antoine'.

'Alex' telephoned a few times but did not come to see me. I told him I was ready but had been unable to find a car. I asked if he was organizing both the weapons transfer and the October 15th operation. He gave me no additional details, but scheduled my trip for the next weekend. I informed 'Antoine'. Then, the day before the trip was scheduled, with no explanation 'Alex' called off the operation.

L.G. He seemed to consider you simply as a logistical resource, both in your role as lawyer and as an activist.

J.P.M. No. Certainly, 'Alex' had not introduced me to any of his comrades but, as far as he was concerned, I was probably in another category: something resembling an independent pawn to be used sparingly wherever he thought me indispensable. I was not Lebanese so there was no reason to involve me in the group's discussions, if there were any. They were probably held in Arabic, anyway. For instance, at one of our meetings at my office, he asked if he might use my telephone to call someone outside France. Since it was a push-button telephone I could not decipher what country he was calling, but he spoke in Arabic, talking in a peremptory tone, almost a monologue, as if he did not intend his orders to be discussed.

L.G. Had your attitude towards 'Alex' changed since you'd entered the Service?

J.P.M. Not really. No sooner had 'Alex' re-established contact with me than I dropped the idea of handling him on my own. The only reason I went to Trieste was to collect as much information as I could, which was justification enough for my actions. I was relieved when the *Piscine* contacted me. I had hoped they would, and had cursed them for leaving me to deal with people I guessed belonged to the FARL on my own. To my mind, just as 'Damien' represented the intelligence service, so 'Alex' was the incarnation of Middle-Eastern terrorism.

The following week was extremely tense. 'Alex' had already cancelled his plans once and was no longer coming to see me. The next weekend was the deadline for what might be a dangerous operation for me. We were coming up to October 15th, and the Service was fully stretched. 'Antoine' confirmed to me that they were on a state of alert, but I had still received no promise of immunity if I were arrested along with 'Alex'.

I spent the entire day of October 15th on the alert. There was a radio on my desk and I listened eagerly to every news bulletin. Nothing. But that didn't make me feel any better, since I could not understand what was happening. Had 'Alex' lied to me? Where was he? What would the *Piscine* think? Would they brand me a liar?

'Antoine' admitted that the Service was disappointed, but they were in no way blaming me. Both the Service and I were growing uneasy. What if we never saw 'Alex' again? Over the next few nights I waited, in vain, at my office for a call or a visit from the one man whose existence justified my being hired as an agent. I panicked, afraid there was no longer any justification for my actions, and that my information was starting to look completely false. Even the weapons transfer had not come about as planned. 'Alex' had truly disappeared.

L.G. Did your status in the Service change?

J.P.M. That's hard to say. During my first meeting with 'Damien' I had made it clear, as I also had at the Security Ministry, that my only intention was preventive action: that is, to contribute to the extent of my ability to the deterrence of any terrorist attacks. 'Alex's' arrest did not interest me as such, even though I knew it was probably inevitable in order to forestall his plans. I was a novice at all this. I didn't know the difference between the DGSE, the security agency that operates outside France, and the DST, internal counter-espionage. The words 'informer' and 'collaborator' horrified me, as I have said. I wanted to serve my country, to protect its people, the faceless crowd. I had no political motives even though I was, and remain, intellectually sympathetic to the Palestinian movement.

In an effort to calm, if not reassure, me 'Antoine' described my exact status in the Service. I was now a Black Agent, a professional person with a full-time job, such as a doctor, a journalist, an engineer, or a lawyer, who under cover of his profession agrees to work almost exclusively for the Service, including carrying out missions and holding himself available at all times. I was not an 'honourable correspondent', of which there are, it seems, some thirty thousand in France alone, who pass on any information they may come across simply out of a sense of civic duty. They are not trained, but merely have a contact in the Service. But a Black Agent is a full member of the Service, working under cover of his profession. The *Piscine* has great need of these people, since they come across information in the course of their daily activities.

Even with 'Alex' gone I did not feel the Service's interest in me had waned. Although inexperienced, I was still their sole link with 'Alex'. I'm not sure the *Piscine* had even been on his track before they contacted me. And their attempt to manoeuvre him into renting a car so they could learn his identity seemed symptomatic, to me, of the level of their knowledge of him.

Also, I had an ace up my sleeve since I was Oriach's lawyer, which was of almost equal interest to them because of his 'revolutionary' friends. From prison, Oriach was corresponding with an impressive number of militants in Belgium, Syria, Italy, Spain, and Germany. Obviously, I've left some out, for what else is there for an imprisoned intellectual to do except write? Oriach was also, possibly, the Service's last hope. It was to obtain his freedom that 'Alex' had planned the two-phase operation. He had asked me to visit Oriach in jail and inform him of those projects, and to assure him of our 'brotherhood in the revolution'! Oriach had seemed surprised to see me, especially since I had refused to represent him at the time of his arrest, in autumn 1982, and had not bothered to answer his letters.

At our meeting I tried to justify my neglect of him by recounting my serious motorcycle accident and my difficult convalescence. Contrary to what has been reported in the media, Oriach and 'Alex' did not know each other and had not established direct contact. But perhaps Oriach had received some sort of signal from the outside about his projected liberation. I had to regain his trust.

Nevertheless, the Service continued to mistrust me since my information had never led to anything concrete and 'they' might have thought either that I had lied, or had warned 'Alex' and forced the FARL underground. Through some tortuous reasoning process, by not handing over the weapons to me 'Alex' was granting me more importance than I had; and the *Piscine*, more logically but with as little foundation, was doing the same. A constant which I observed was that my thoughts and attitudes were much further from 'Alex's' than his and my contacts' in the Service were from each other. Which is normal, given that one of the first rules of strategy is to try to put yourself in your enemy's place.

|4| **LYONS**

After the cancellation of 'Operation Gardening' and the non-event of 15 October, 'Alex' failed to contact Jean-Paul Mazurier again. As the days passed, Mazurier became seriously worried that he might have seen the last of him. Then, on 28 October, he received a message from an examining magistrate in Lyons. A man named Saadi Abdelkader had been arrested there for the possession of forged passports, and had named Mazurier as his lawyer.

The name was unfamiliar, but the man was not. It was 'Alex', soon to be publicly identified as Georges Ibrahim Abdallah, head of the FARL.

Jean-Paul Mazurier 'Alex' still had not reappeared, October was drawing to a close, and I was eaten up with worry. What error had I made, what carelessness had caused him to flee? How could I re-establish the link? On the afternoon of October 28th I received a registered letter posted from Lyons. An examining magistrate there was writing to inform me that he had ordered the detention of one Saadi Abdelkader, who had named me as his lawyer. I had no idea who he was, but the Arabic name aroused my suspicions. Telephoning the lawyer who had assisted 'my' client in the examining magistrate's office, I asked him to describe Saadi Abdelkader. My forebodings became a reality when he said: 'Well, he has a beard . . .'

Laurent Gally It was 'Alex', and you would now have to deal with him in this new situation?

J.P.M. Yes. The descriptions were identical, but what was

'Alex' doing in Lyons? I was not surprised he was facing charges under a different identity, since the man I knew as 'Alex' was 'Georges' to Hamami, and so on. It is a basic rule that militant revolutionaries have several passports, and in fact 'Alex' had been charged with the possession and use of forged passports. In the course of their investigation the police learned that the Algerian passport in the name of Saadi Abdelkader, an Algerian citizen, was real, which would prove an embarrassment for Algiers. On the other hand, the Maltese passport in the name of Michael Kanary was a forgery.

But that was not the worst of it. The photocopied form the magistrate sent me indicated that 'Alex' had also been indicted for 'criminal associations', a vague legal term lawyers dread. When the legal system decides to throw the book at someone who is suspected of the worst crimes, but against whom there is no hard evidence, he is indicted on that charge, 'criminal associations'. Although it might have also meant that 'Alex' had not been arrested alone and that, perhaps, some of his 'comrades' were also in prison. In any case, I would have to leave immediately. Telephoning the Service, I reported to my superiors. My contact seemed both flabbergasted and relieved that 'Alex's' trail had grown warm again, even though he was in jail, and that he had immediately named me as his defence counsel. I was given no particular instructions, except to go and see 'Alex' as quickly as possible.

L.G. Had you expected him to be arrested?

J.P.M. Not at all. It was in nobody's interest, and certainly not that of the Service, if their intention was to pick up his trail, and above all to learn more about the plot he was hatching. 'Alex' had never mentioned Lyons, and I began to wonder if part of his network might not be based there, where he had by chance, and so stupidly, been arrested.

I took the high-speed train to Lyons, overcome by the idea that his projected operations might go forward without me, that I'd be shut out of the action, and would have to go back to being what I had never wanted to be: the lawyer for a member, if not the chief, of the FARL. Not to mention the inopportune publicity to which I would be subjected, protected only – but for how long? – by the anonymity of the name Saadi Abdelkader.

Waiting for 'Alex' in the visitors' room of Lyons' St Paul Prison, I had the curious sensation that from now on I would be the one who would choose the day, and the time, of our visits. The emotion was something akin to vengeance, after having spent so many anxious hours waiting for him. But here, too, I was wrong. The trip to Lyons would almost immediately become a daily chore imposed on me by the needs of the Service.

'Alex' didn't seem to have been particularly affected by his situation and seemed to be taking it as a huge joke. He explained to me that it was all a mistake. He had obviously let the police officers know it too, during his detention, disclosing that he had just moved the members of his network out of France, and that Paris had nothing more to fear from them since French interests were no longer threatened. He represented himself, as the press reported at the time, as one of the members of the RMAU, the Revolutionary Movement for Arab Unity. According to him, the aim of the group was to determine which projects, hostile to the Palestinian cause, emanated from American or Zionist groups based in France. Reading the preliminary charges, it immediately became apparent to me that from the very beginning of his interrogation the investigators suspected 'Alex' of belonging to, or even leading, the mysterious Lebanese Armed Revolutionary Faction. That was another point I would have to clear up: what made the police so certain?

L.G. So from the beginning you suspected that 'Alex's' arrest was a set-up? Had you ever heard him say anything about evacuating his terrorist network?

J.P.M. I knew nothing of the details of his arrest. He said nothing about it until later, during some of my visits. But from the moment, about two weeks earlier, that he asked me to take charge of the arsenal he intended to move from its Paris hiding place, I suspected that 'Alex', and possibly the rest of the FARL, were thinking of leaving France. If only temporarily, long enough to carry out the October 15th operation. And perhaps for even longer, since 'Alex' had made it very clear that the weapons could remain hidden for two or three years if need be.

I did not know where his comrades were until he himself told me, on 29 October 1984. 'You must telephone this number as quickly as you can,' he said, his gaze growing more intense, 'and tell the comrades I've been arrested. They'll know what to do.'

I agreed without even looking at the number scribbled on the piece of paper he slipped into my hand. At last! I was now in possession of new data that, for the first time, would allow the Service to track down FARL members, and perhaps even round them up.

After leaving the prison, I studied the telephone number, which was somewhere in Italy. After my trip to Trieste, I recognized the area code. I telephoned Paris. After hearing of the assignment 'Alex' had given me, 'Antoine' ordered me to return to my office and await further orders.

L.G. This is the third time you brought a breakthrough in the case to the *Piscine*, even though the first two didn't work out.

J.P.M. Yes, but this time it would be the Service itself that let the chance slip through its fingers. On my arrival in Paris, 'Antoine' met me and told me that, as usual, I was to obey 'Alex's' orders and make the call. In order not to arouse 'Alex's' suspicions, the Service had not yet installed any microphones in my office. There wasn't even a tap on my telephone. For the same reason, and so as not to put me in danger, no agent had even photographed 'Alex' as he arrived for our meetings. Which means that the first photographs the *Piscine* had of him were the police mug-shots taken at the time of his arrest.

But this time 'Antoine' brought along two technicians to record my call to Italy. It was very brief. I dialled the number, the phone rang twice and then a woman's voice said: '*Pronto.*'

'Hello,' I said, 'do you speak French?' She said yes. 'I am *Maître* Mazurier, 'Alex's' lawyer in Paris. He asked me to tell you he was arrested in Lyons five days ago. I've just been to see him in jail. He wants you to take the necessary precautions.'

I intentionally left pauses between my sentences so the woman might ask me questions. Nothing. In a blank voice she said 'Thank you', as if she weren't at all surprised, and then hung up without saying another word.

I looked at 'Antoine', wondering what to do next. He explained that the Service had traced the phone number to the town of Ostia, the seaside town outside Rome, and to an apartment they had managed to identify. But they had no intention of stirring up a hornets' nest by arresting the supporting players, which would have set off a general alarm inside the group, and could only lead them to suspect me. The Service's strategy was to stick with 'Alex', since they had concluded he was, indeed, the head of the FARL. The telephone call to Ostia appeared to confirm that.

L.G. Had the *Piscine* informed the Italian security services?

J.P.M. Certainly not. And this was quite fair, as the Italians might have decided to raid the place. It was happening on their territory and they could not be counted on to take the *Piscine*'s tactical plans into account. Some time later, when DIGOS, the Italian secret service, arrested the group of Lebanese who were planning an attack on the American embassy in Rome, the arrests were made in an apartment in Ostia, although I could never learn if it was the same place. As a rule, once a safe house is 'burned' it is never used again.

I can't discount the possibility that the Service did inform their Italian counterparts afterwards, but without telling them a terrorist group had been allowed to evacuate its people. There are a thousand ways of presenting the facts. 'They' later told me the Italians searched the apartment some two months after the event, but found nothing. What I don't know is, was one of the Service's Rome operatives warned long enough in advance of my call to be able to set up surveillance on the apartment and at least to learn how many militants moved out, if not photograph them?

L.G. Did the DGSE have a tendency to try to handle the FARL case on its own?

J.P.M. I believe they were obliged to. The next time I saw 'Alex' he told me, rather sheepishly, how he had been arrested. He had been on his way back to retrieve the rental security deposit he had paid on one of the safe-house apartments in Lyons, and believed he was being followed by Mossad agents. I couldn't tell if he was afraid, or annoyed, but as the press later reported, he went into a police station and demanded protection against the men following him. But it turned out the men were French security police, members of the DST, and they immediately began to question him.

The story seems funny, even absurd, but it does illustrate the problems the Service had in dealing with this affair. Firstly, there was probably no co-operation between the *Piscine* and the DST regarding 'Alex'. No doubt the *Piscine* did not want it known that, thanks to me, it had managed to infiltrate someone next to 'Alex'. That's understandable, except perhaps at the very highest levels, because even within the *Piscine*, most agents knew nothing of my role, and probably took me for a lawyer in league with the terrorists. My true role was kept secret for security reasons, and that implies a very strict system of isolation.

Secondly, the DST had its own sources of information in this affair. Had they put them together independently, or did they have the help of foreign intelligence services? Many theories have been put forward, and it is not up to me to settle the question. Cursing his own carelessness, even 'Alex' himself did not exclude the possibility that he might have been followed from my office when he came to see me after my return from Trieste. Since the DGSE knew about the trip, the DST might have learned about it as well, perhaps from the agents who tried to scare me off in Italy. In any case, its sources of information were excellent, extending far beyond what could be learned simply by tailing someone. And when 'Alex' mentioned the RMAU, neither the local Lyons police nor even the local criminal investigations department could have recognized that the movement he was describing resembled a misleadingly moderate version of the FARL. I believe that during his first interrogation 'Alex' may suddenly have found himself face-to-face with an officer – French, or Israeli? – who could read him so well that he was forced to invent that tale about the RMAU.

L.G. Do you have any solid evidence to support that theory?

J.P.M. Yes, the interrogation transcript mentions the confrontation, but without giving the person's name. My intuition is reinforced by the fact that, knowing he was being followed, 'Alex' demanded French police protection. Which means he thought he had nothing to fear from the French police; quite the opposite.

According to what he told me, I don't believe 'Alex' was physically afraid of the men who had been following him for three or four days. His 'mission' was over, he had moved out his network – under the eyes of the DST? – and settled up accounts at all his safe houses. Was he following someone else's instructions? His self-assurance with the French police, his feelings of immunity even during my first visit to him in jail (at that time he believed he would be released quickly) suggest that an agreement had been reached.

Between who and whom? That remains a mystery. But it would not have been the first time such a thing had occurred. There have been press reports of a secret 1983 meeting between Joseph Franceschi, France's Security Minister, and Abou Nidal, one of the most famous Palestinian terrorists. The meeting reportedly led to a pact in which Abou Nidal promised his forces would not perpetrate attacks in France. Similarly, Pierre Marion, director of the *Piscine* from 1981 to 1983, recently revealed an almost identical agreement he made at that time with Rifaat al-Assad, brother of the Syrian president, for a truce in all activities against French interests.

L.G. Following that logic, couldn't 'Alex' have been directly concerned in one or another of those agreements? Or might he himself have made a similar pact or, inversely, have been a lieutenant of one of the Arab political figures you have just mentioned?

J.P.M. All that is part of a group of theories no one, in my opinion, has ever analyzed properly. After reading the case file, and taking into consideration 'Alex's' initially optimistic attitude during his first two weeks in jail, I concluded that his arrest had been quite fortuitous. When he took refuge in the police station the DST agents following him were forced to make a spur-of-the-moment decision. Once 'Alex' had entered the lion's den, could they simply identify themselves and tell him that everything was all right, that they were just following him to ensure his personal safety, then let him go again? Did they have precise orders about what to do if 'Alex' spotted them? Those agents were not of very high rank, unlike the head of the DST office in Lyons, who was there in person when they questioned 'Alex'. Another possibility is that the executive officers of the DST were out to 'get' 'Alex'. His stay in Lyons might have been one of their last opportunities to apprehend him, if the DST had also learned of the operation planned for October 15th and intended to 'neutralize' 'Alex' before he left France.

Lyons is not a very practical place in which to carry out that sort of operation. Everyone in the legal profession knows Paris is where the most important cases are handled and that the government, either quietly or openly, involves itself in them through the public prosecutors, who are subject to the Justice Ministry. 'Alex's' being arrested in Lyons automatically meant that the case would be given to an examining magistrate who was not a specialist in terrorist cases and this was the first time Mademoiselle Kleinmann, the examining magistrate who handled the Lyons part of 'Alex's' case, had been given a major dossier. The result of this was that after the March 1986 general election, and the shift in political power,* Parliament immediately passed an internal security law calling for all terrorist cases to be handled directly from Paris.

L.G. You have not discussed either of the non-aggression pacts which might have included 'Alex', nor his possible membership of various organizations based in the Middle East, in Lebanon or Syria.

J.P.M. It is up to the government to say whether there was, or was not, an agreement concerning 'Alex' and the activities of the FARL. We'll probably never know, in view of later developments in the affair, unless historians are allowed access to the government's archives. Was 'Alex' obeying someone else's orders? After having met him more than a hundred times in four years, I don't think so. I have described him as displaying the qualities of a leader; in my presence he never mentioned any of the other well-known international terrorists except to criticize them. For example, some time later, speaking of Abou Nidal, he said: 'One cannot be part of the power structure and remain a revolutionary.' That was his final judgement on the man. On the other hand, I can very well imagine 'Alex' submitting to some sort of agreement,

* RPR (*Rassemblement pour la République*), the Gaullist party, led by Jacques Chirac, took power from the Socialist party.

even one made with a government, if the conditions it imposed on him tended towards what he judged to be the interests of the Palestinian cause. Many times he said to me, as a *credo*: 'Palestine is the lever of the revolution.'

L.G. At that time, were you handling 'Alex's' defence on your own?

J.P.M. Yes, since the lawyer assigned to him when he appeared before the examining magistrate had resigned from the case. He was later replaced by *Maître* Boyer, a former Jesuit priest, who 'Alex' named because he felt it more convenient to have a local lawyer too. Once I entered the prison visitors' room just as Boyer was leaving. Greeting me, he asked if I intended to allow the case to drag on since, with me there, 'Alex' was refusing to answer the examining magistrate's questions. I made a vague gesture. Boyer added: 'In any case, he told me this will all be settled very quickly through diplomatic channels.' Surprised, I glanced at 'Alex' questioningly, and saw him blush, embarrassed at having let slip something that, theoretically, I was the only one to know. Since it seemed that diplomatic negotiations had begun, I was even more convinced that his arrest had been an error. But he offered no further explanation of the matter.

'Alex' had named me as his defence counsel the first time he appeared before the examining magistrate, and told me he had tried to present this choice as being an innocuous one, almost fortuitous: 'I know the name of a Paris lawyer. It's Maurien, I think, or Masurien. No, I remember: Jean-Paul Mazurier.' Of course the magistrate had never heard of me, nor had the Lyons prosecutor's office.

A few weeks later, when 'Alex' had lost hope of being released immediately, we began to wonder if it wouldn't be better to hire an additional lawyer so as to give the police, and the press, someone on whom to focus. We, I repeat, *we*, immediately thought of *Maître* Jacques Vergès, a very talented member of the Bar and the almost obligatory counsel to all 'revolutionaries' imprisoned in France. Vergès is a great orator, a clever legal mind, and incredibly good at using the media. 'Alex' asked my help in writing a letter to *Maître* Vergès, soliciting his aid. A few days later, I telephoned my colleague.

'I hear you've been named by a man called Saadi Abdelkader. What do you intend to do?'

'I'm going to look at the file in Lyons, and ask for permission to visit him. Why do you ask?'

'I thought, if you like, we could visit our client together.'

'Does that mean that you, too, have been named? In that case, as a courtesy towards you, there is no question of my taking part in the case. I'll write to your client and tell him he has made an excellent choice and that two lawyers, for one simple case of forged passports, seems unjustified to me.'

'Perhaps we ought to join forces. I think there's more to this than the official charges suggest. I'm not certain I can handle it alone.'

'I'm sorry. No matter what sort of case this may be, you've already been named to represent the client. I have no intention of encroaching on your territory, and will not take the case.'

L.G. Are you certain 'Alex' and Vergès didn't know each other? And that naming him co-counsel wasn't part of your client's strategy.

J.P.M. Yes, I do believe they had not been in contact, although I later learned that 'Alex' approached him again, through his comrades. But for the moment Vergès would not enter the case, which seems to prove – assuming one does not suspect them both of being extremely Machiavellian – that he knew nothing about what was happening beneath the surface in this affair.

L.G. But, on the other hand, wasn't it dangerous for 'Alex' to hire *Maître* Vergès as his defence counsel since he was known as the lawyer for militants involved in terrorism, while your client was presenting himself as an intellectual?

J.P.M. When he finally understood that his arrest was not merely a misunderstanding, and that he would not be released quickly, 'Alex' realized that sooner or later his case would become public, which is what happened. At that point Vergès would be able to play his full role. Of course, the media have pointed out that *Maître* Vergès defended both Bruno Bréguet and Magdalena Kopp, alleged 'friends of Carlos'. And, inevitably, in the public's mind Alex became associated with Carlos. But that would have happened, no matter what. In any case 'Alex' had never talked to me about Carlos.

L.G. At what point did *Maître* Vergès become 'Alex's' lawyer?

J.P.M. As soon as the entire affair became public. The weekend before Christmas 1984, a weekly magazine published an exclusive: 'Alex's' true identity. His real name was Georges Ibrahim Abdallah and he was identified as the head of the FARL. The article, which covered everything, including five or six successive aliases 'Alex' had used, was reprinted everywhere in France.

So on the following Monday, December 24th, *Maître* Vergès went to St Paul Prison to meet his potential client. After all, a lawyer's clientele depends a great deal on his public appearances and media coverage. Besides, the fact that he acted so quickly after 'Alex's' identity was divulged might also mean that *Maître* Vergès was readily accepting the challenge of a public, and extremely sensitive, affair.

What puzzled me most was who had informed the press. Journalist friends confirmed what at first was only an idea: that the DST had 'handed over' the man who would now be known to everyone in France as Abdallah.

L.G. Perhaps, but to what end? Some sources have suggested that perhaps Abdallah was a banana skin the DST was slipping under the Socialist party's feet.

J.P.M. The report of his true identity – for that one is real, and we were all becoming a little lost among all of 'Alex-Georges'' aliases – led me to reconsider the way in which he had been arrested in Lyons. What if the government had not wanted him arrested? Perhaps all the leaks to the press were simply meant to put the best possible face on the police's actions. But then why had they waited two months? Had the leak come from inside the DST? It's possible, but it would have been the second error that organization had committed in the case, the first being the Lyons arrest.

The theory which has the DST deliberately embarrassing the government does hold up, but I have no idea of whether it was for political or internal police reasons. What appears to be a constant since 1974, and particularly since the release of Abou Daud, the Palestinian arrested in France and wanted in West Germany for organizing the massacre of the Israeli athletes during the 1976

Munich Olympics, is that the authorities had no desire to keep in custody such awkward prisoners as the heads of Middle-Eastern terrorist groups.

L.G. Once Abdallah was identified, and imprisoned, didn't you ever learn anything about the diplomatic contacts aimed at freeing him, at the end of 1984 or the beginning of 1985?

J.P.M. No, never. He would not tell me about a visit he received from Algerian emissaries until April 1985, one month afterwards, and then only to assure me he had refused to see them. Their visit was tied to the Gilles Sidney Peyroles affair, the French diplomat who had been kidnapped in Lebanon* and was being held by the FARL in hopes of exchanging him for Abdallah. There, too, the DST may have deliberately torpedoed the planned exchange, as if someone highly placed was determined Abdallah should remain in jail. But I was just an ordinary agent of the Service, inventing these possible political scenarios for myself.

L.G. How did Abdallah behave before the examining magistrate?

J.P.M. Mademoiselle Kleinmann was very aware that she was dealing with an important case, something rare for a magistrate at the beginning of her career. She did everything she could to fulfil her mandate, unfortunately by tending mainly towards the prosecution's point of view. Thus it was that she sent a request to Lebanon for an investigation to be made, with consequences which were, perhaps, disastrous for French interests there. The Phalangists, who still controlled most of the government, now knew that Abdallah, probably one of their worst political enemies, was sitting back and waiting, safe in a French jail. This may have led to political negotiations aimed at simply extraditing him to Beirut after going through the formality of a trial. This hypothesis has been discussed in the media.

Naturally, 'Alex' did nothing to co-operate with the magistrate, but wrapped himself in haughty silence until his trial. I only saw him laugh once, and this was noted in the official transcript of his interrogations, when the young woman magistrate presented him

* On 24 March 1985.

with what she seemed to consider a decisive piece of evidence against him. His fingerprints had been found on a bottle of typewriter correcting fluid in the apartment the FARL used as a weapons cache. On his part, Abdallah always displayed an extremely political, almost accusatory attitude towards the judge's position. He was refusing to answer not Mademoiselle Kleinmann, but the magistrate 'carrying out the orders of the French State, a factual ally of imperialism and Zionism,' as he put it. He denied, *a priori*, her ability to be juridically independent.

|5| THE MESSENGER

During Abdallah's first weeks of imprisonment, Jean-Paul Mazurier was virtually his sole link with the outside world. It was a situation which the DGSE were anxious to exploit. Acting on their instructions, Mazurier agreed to take messages from Abdallah for the other members of the FARL. He telephoned the coded messages to a woman who called herself 'Nathalie' – the woman Abdallah had ordered to evacuate the Ostia safe house. At the same time he passed them on to the DGSE, who found their contents very interesting indeed.

Jean-Paul Mazurier It was now the beginning of November 1984, and the Service was still angry about 'Alex's' arrest. Nothing had happened on October 15th, or in the weeks following it. 'Alex's' disappearance before his arrest had put off indefinitely the transfer of the FARL's Paris weapons arsenal and, with it, all possibility of establishing contact with other members of the group. In order not to arouse 'Alex's' suspicions, the Service had permitted me to evacuate the Ostia safe house. Now 'Alex' remained our sole link with the FARL, although we were aware that he was also the biggest prize. The strategy was simple. Now that he was, theoretically, cut off from the outside world he would have to call on me in order to maintain contact with his group and, no matter what the cost, I would have to command his trust.

Laurent Gally Was 'Alex', since at this point he was not yet officially 'Abdallah', completely cut off from the outside world?

J.P.M. Yes and no. Like most prisoners he managed to find a way to communicate with the outside, but by passing messages out of prison rather than receiving any, which was riskier. Several months later 'Alex' would tell me that some time in December 1984 he managed to send out three cassettes containing hours of instructions and battle orders that he recorded in his prison cell. They went out with the complicity of a prison boss, a Corsican gangster who controlled what went on within the prison population. 'Alex' had even received confirmation that his messages had reached their destination!

I have no idea what he ordered his comrades to do on those tapes. Perhaps he was already planning to have himself exchanged for a Frenchman kidnapped in Lebanon, three months before Gilles Peyroles, the French diplomat, was taken hostage? It's a mystery. It may seem incredible to the general public but prison walls are not impenetrable. Some prisoners come back in, others go free; the Arab prisoners stand together, no matter what their political opinions. As a lawyer I regard it as normal that it's possible to get things done in prison, if only occasionally and if one is not being held in solitary confinement. In 'Alex's' case, considering the minimal charges against him, there was no justification for keeping him in isolation.

L.G. Was that the only leak you found in the Abdallah case?

J.P.M. No, but I don't think it changed a thing as far as the basis of the affair was concerned. In 1986, Abdallah described in detail how he had asked a Syrian who was being released on parole to carry several letters to his group.

L.G. 'Alex' couldn't continue leading his group from inside prison, could he?

J.P.M. No, and the *Piscine* were very unhappy about it since they could no longer learn what the terrorists, angered perhaps by the arrest of their leader, were planning to do. It was at this moment that 'they' asked me to act as a channel of information, carrying messages almost daily between 'Georges', as I now called him, and the outside.

Georges had ordered me to do this at our first meeting in the visitors' room, when asking me to telephone Ostia, but the scenario changed somewhat once I had carried out that assignment. During each of my visits through the entire month of November 1984 he dictated to me some dozen vivid but unintelligible phrases, coded messages. Each afternoon I would take the train back to Paris, return to my office punctually at six and remain there until eight in the evening, waiting for a call from the person to whom I was to transmit the messages. She would then dictate other messages for Georges, answers to his own messages of the day before, I suppose, and I would return to Lyons the next morning. All this forced me to make constant trips back and forth to Lyons, which were not at all justified by the examining magistrate's progress in the case. Yet no one, at the Palais de Justice, or at St Paul Prison, seemed surprised at my excess of professional integrity.

L.G. Are you certain no judge in Lyons was aware of your true role?

J.P.M. Absolutely certain. I am sure that the Paris magistrate in whom I had confided, and who I still saw from time to time, had said nothing to any of his colleagues. In Lyons, Mademoiselle Kleinmann, the examining magistrate, was openly disdainful towards me, although icily polite. Inside the Palais de Justice itself, I am certain I was thought of as a lawyer for terrorists, if not a terrorist lawyer. But there was no proof against me and, the position of counsel for the defence being rather a protected one, I was able to bring all of Georges' messages out of the prison without once being searched, since lawyers only pass through a metal detector. Naturally, it was illegal for me to be carrying letters from a jailed client, but the theory is quite often different from the practice. This is for simple humanitarian reasons, since the Penal Code even forbids a lawyer to give a prisoner's family news of the state of his health.

L.G. Was the Service able to decode those messages?

J.P.M. Of course, and very quickly or they would not have allowed me to continue playing this part. The *Piscine*'s cryptographers took some time to decode them at first, but after that it became child's play. So much so that in 1985 they were translating messages Georges was receiving from the outside while he, weakened or exhausted by his time in custody, began to lose all memory of certain key words in his own code, as he admitted to me.

I was the only one who couldn't read the phrases! It was the rule that the Service did not tell me what was in the messages so that that knowledge did not influence my behaviour. Naturally, I tried to work out the sense of the messages, and Georges knew it. One day he asked me if I understood a phrase I was supposed to transmit, and I guessed at a fairly obvious translation of it. He smiled, satisfied: 'You have a logical mind,' he said. 'That's good. Even if your office is bugged, it doesn't matter. They'll analyze it the way you did and be led in the wrong direction.'

L.G. Do you have any actual phrases from Abdallah's messages?

J.P.M. I retain vague memories of them, but no physical traces since simple prudence demanded I give the Service everything Georges dictated, without making any photocopies. I did not want there to be any hitches, if investigators should come to search my office. Such things happen rarely, but still it is always a possibility if one is suspected of conspiracy. And I could not forget that the DST and the DGSE had very different attitudes towards this case.

I remember once my secretary entered my office without knocking; the message I was about to dictate was in plain sight. Glancing at it automatically, she smiled and said: 'Oh, have you started writing poetry?' Actually, Georges' coded messages sounded like those heard over the BBC in World War II, during the Resistance period and then at the time of the Normandy Invasion in 1944, or like the unciphered messages anyone might send if he were trying to camouflage his meaning.

The most classic phrase I can remember was 'the key to the treasure'. Was Georges referring to money, or weapons? Once he mentioned 'the eye of the pigeon', with no explanation of what that bird embodied. Another, more politically oriented phrase said, 'One does not compromise with the big animal, and even less with him who holds the oil of Mecca.' I deduced that the 'big animal' had to be Syria, and the one 'who holds the oil of Mecca' might have been Iran, but that is only a guess. Saudi Arabia is too obvious a solution to that puzzle, and as far as I know it was not involved in the affair. Commenting on that phrase, Georges tried to explain it to me using another maxim: 'I came into it red, and I will come out of it red,' thus assuring me that he valued his status as a militant revolutionary above all else, and was not disposed to purchase his freedom by becoming a vassal of any one of the Middle-Eastern countries supposedly supporting him. For my part, I do not rule out the possibility that the Service, or even the French government, might have been using those messages to weigh the results they might expect from diplomatic contacts between Paris and the various countries.

In his messages Abdallah did not often talk of politics, but instead sent directives to action, addressing himself particularly to one or another member of his group. Thus, after having received letters from Lebanon, he dictated the following message: 'I do not want to talk to anyone but my confidante. It is in her, and her alone, that I have confidence.' The message was clear, probably hammering home a point and confirming the decision-making powers of someone within his group who might have been in the process of losing that power.

L.G. Do you know who that confidante was?

J.P.M. Yes, since I was dictating Georges' messages over the telephone to a woman. She had introduced herself as 'Nathalie', and on the evening after my second meeting with Georges, after he was jailed, asked me for 'news of the health of my big brother, who is in the hospital'. And she added, in an attempt to put me completely at my ease: 'I was the one you called the other day . . .' I had recognized her voice as that of the woman who answered the telephone at Ostia. She would call me between six and eight, practically every evening.

From his prison cell, Georges appeared to be managing the problems of each of his collaborators. One of his first messages concerned 'The Englishwoman'. 'Take care of her,' he wrote, 'I love her like a sister. She has nothing to do with this.' Later I would learn that he was referring to Joséphine Abdo Sarkis, a Lebanese woman who spoke perfect English. Generally, Georges was as explicit as possible when dealing with the personal problems of one comrade or another, but when it came to giving strategic orders, or instructions for actions to be taken, he coded his messages.

Another question is, was he communicating with *Maître* Vergès? In the middle of November 1984 Georges dictated a message that read: 'Tell the half-Asian to come and see Kasem.' *Maître* Vergès' family is of both Asian and La Réunion island descent; Kasem turned out to be one of the many names Abdallah had used years earlier, on the island of Cyprus. This happened at around the time Vergès told me he would not take on the case.

Another message was more cryptic: 'Raymonda must stay with the brother of the wife of the little bastard. It is up to my father, and only him, to take care of her. If she wants to fly away, let her.' That text might have concerned half a Lebanese village, or the internal structure of a group within the FARL, 'little bastard' being the literal translation of an Arabic term of affection. The French phrases Georges dictated were often rather awkward since they had to correspond to a precise grammatical structure when retranslated into Arabic.

L.G. Did he ever discuss his family, or his brothers?

J.P.M. Never. Once, when his eyes or teeth were bothering him, he told me his father had taught him something about medicine. In the spring of 1985, he made brief mention of his 'little sister' being kidnapped and tortured by the Lebanese Phalangists. I don't know if she was actually his sister, or a young militant particularly close to him, but the episode occurred at the time the French sent an international rogatory commission to Beirut. That is, an official request for information which gave the Lebanese police a pretext for taking action against Georges' family and friends.

The media have expounded on the 'Abdallah clan' and the villages of Kubayat and Andakat, in which almost all the FARL militants are supposedly concentrated. Georges never mentioned those names to me, saying simply: 'It's reassuring to know they're such idiots. They forget about the chicken and the egg.'

L.G. Were you able to determine from where 'Nathalie' was calling?

J.P.M. I don't know. I had spoken to her last in Ostia, on the evening of October 29th. She might have taken a plane, or found refuge in another Italian safe house, or in a neighbouring European country. When I was studying the case files I noticed that, according to police investigations, the FARL were extraordinarily mobile and could very quickly travel thousands of miles for the needs of their cause. Revolutionaries take the plane as often as businessmen do.

My telephone contacts with 'Nathalie' lasted about a month, punctuated by trips to see her in person. Then she did not telephone me again until 8 August 1985. This means that Georges must have discovered another way of reaching the outside, using other messengers, but no doubt on an irregular basis.

L.G. Exactly how useful were these messages to the Service?

J.P.M. It all depends on the decoding and the practical uses to which they were put, as well as the results obtained in the field. My responsibility was to transmit the parts of a puzzle which was being put together, a piece at a time. It was certainly of some use since the *Piscine*'s trust in me was becoming more and more evident. Proof of this was the appreciable increase in my monthly allowance. My handler also took me to meet a certain 'Monsieur Jean', whom I was later told was a psychologist. This means they were still testing me with a view to giving me other tasks.

L.G. Conversely, was Abdallah satisfied with your work?

J.P.M. As far as he was concerned I was merely doing a militant's 'normal' work. Yet he was very concerned for my safety. At the beginning of December 1984, in an effort to make him open up to me, I told him I thought I was being followed. He asked me to describe the suspects and I gave him a description of the men who had tried to scare me off in Trieste. Georges then suggested I apply for Syrian and Lebanese visas, saying I might be able to learn something about the militants' way of life there and possibly find work, for example in the visa bureau at the French consulate! The proposition might appear naive, or too obvious, but I was his only lawyer at the time, he had an almost visceral need of me, and my safety was essential to him. Without me he would no longer have his daily communication channel.

I do believe he truly feared for me since, he explained, Mossad's tactics were to try to eliminate each unit within an enemy group.

Therefore, I must have seemed to him to be directly in the line of fire, yet he still would not provide me with a 'contact' in Paris. On the contrary, when I was refused a Lebanese visa, he suggested I take a week's holiday to forget about the people who might be following me.

L.G. After Abdallah's arrest, you never had any contacts in Paris?

J.P.M. I think I might have done, towards the end of November, when he had been in jail for a month and was coming to realize that this was no misunderstanding. According to the bits of information the Service was giving me in order to keep me satisfied, Abdallah had first sent a series of orders to his comrades, instructing them to remain calm, and moderate in their behaviour. Later, when he saw matters more realistically, he understood he would have to do something positive in order to regain his freedom. This led to stronger messages, as 'Nathalie' confirmed to me over the phone one evening. It was 22 November 1984, and she told me that 'someone' would be coming to my office at eleven the next morning. Having recorded the conversation, I informed the Service and 'they' decided to transform me into a walking microphone. We set a meeting for the next morning at nine, at my house near the Place des Vosges.

The next morning, besides the drunk who often slept in a nearby doorway, I noticed more tramps than usual on the street. My handler told me they were agents who were there to make sure the coast was clear. The *Piscine* had abandoned its initial idea of using microphones, deciding it would be too dangerous for me, but were confident I could memorize everything that was said. I telephoned my girlfriend to tell her she could have my car – a recent acquisition that had been unavailable to 'Alex' at the time of 'Operation Gardening' – as she had planned. She informed me that just after I left someone had telephoned. A man had asked for me and, when told I had gone, had hesitated, then said: 'Tell him "Alex" called.'

I was convinced it was my eleven o'clock contact being called off, and perhaps the voice had wanted to change the meeting to another time. But how to reach him? The Service instructed me to wait for him in my office, almost as a matter of form. As expected he did not appear and, unfortunately, never called again.

L.G. Taking into consideration both that mysterious man, and 'Nathalie's' telephone calls, everything seems to indicate that the FARL were no longer in Paris, or only came there occasionally.

J.P.M. That is what I thought. After his arrest 'Alex' must have sent out general instructions to act cautiously, since he had no idea what the people who spotted him actually knew. I had proof that 'Nathalie' was somewhere outside France, and the comrade who stood me up was also probably no longer based in Paris or he would have called again that same day. At the time of his arrest, 'Alex' had coolly stated that the FARL were leaving France.

L.G. Given that you were not allowed to know the meaning of the decoded messages, how did you discern the group's change of tactics?

J.P.M. As I have said, there were two sorts of messages, coded and personal. Also, I could see in Georges' eyes what he was feeling when he received the messages, to say nothing of hearing his personal comments. At each of my visits I could try to get a sense of the atmosphere, and that was about all. But that is what the Service wanted, as I was expected to remain as neutral as I possibly could. So I played the role of postman, sneaking glances at the rather special postcards entrusted to me.

Still, I knew that important things were happening on another level. One day Georges dictated a message for 'Nathalie': 'He is in good health. He received the two letters from Samuelsa. It is she he trusts. Have her keep the little ones with her father, and not travel much. Once a month is enough.' The general sense of this message may appear comprehensible, but it is the details that count, in order to be able to act. Were the 'little ones' terrorists, or weapons? Who was Samuelsa? He had made me repeat the name several times to be sure that I understood it. Where did the father live, in Lebanon, or in Europe? Was he a person or an organization? And from where had the two letters come? I was totally puzzled although, no doubt, the Service was not.

Then, perhaps, the prison administration finally realized that Georges was receiving messages from outside. Early in January

1985, he asked me to bring him a linen pullover, I think it was, the next day. When I returned, bringing a common, everyday sweater, I was told, without explanation, that my client had been transferred to the Santé Prison, in Paris, the previous night. I was filled with misgivings. Had they become afraid of an escape attempt because of that sweater? Were they expecting him to take it apart and re-plait it into a rope? Had they bugged the visitors' room? Did they suspect me, even vaguely, of helping him in a possible escape?

L.G. Besides the messages and letters, did Abdallah receive much news from the outside?

J.P.M. Like most prisoners he read some daily newspapers, but only French ones, unlike Joséphine Abdo who, imprisoned in Italy, could subscribe to Lebanese newspapers. And Georges, who thanks to the public repercussions of his case had quickly become a celebrity inside the prison, was pretty much on his own. He was in jail alongside common criminals with whom he could not discuss politics, and from whom he could hardly hope to learn any news. But he received letters from Joséphine Abdo, written in Arabic and first read by the censor, that supplied him with information about developments in the Near East.

What served to isolate him most were the Service's actions. At the beginning, Abdallah called the DGSE the 'little boys'. But he quickly changed his tune and in January 1985 was no longer giving me messages, since my contacts with 'Nathalie' had been cut off. The reason was that it was impossible for the Service both to have messages flowing between the group's various leaders, and to act on them. Because each action, based as it was on the information contained in these messages, would logically cause the flow to dry up . . . by casting suspicion on me.

For a while Georges regarded me as a security risk and when, at his request, I described my daily life to him, reproached me for my carelessness. Then, although he would not tell me this until six months later after I had been 'cleared', he asked his comrades to investigate me. I never noticed anything, and do not know if the FARL had me under surveillance in Paris. True professionals, they were much more wary than I was.

|6| **JACQUELINE ESBER**

As well as passing on messages to 'Nathalie' by telephone, Jean-Paul Mazurier had more demanding duties to perform in his dual role of terrorist sympathizer and undercover agent. On 31 October, a week after Abdallah's arrest, 'Nathalie' had phoned Mazurier with instructions to meet her at Rome airport the following day. It was the first of three nerve-wracking trips abroad which he had to make during November.

Before long, Mazurier would discover 'Nathalie's' true identity. She was Jacqueline Esber, a notorious FARL terrorist wanted in France for murder.

Jean-Paul Mazurier On 31 October 1984 I was deep in an armed robber's case file, my everyday work, when the telephone rang.

'Hello. You must come to Rome tomorrow. I'll meet you at the airport. Take the plane that arrives late in the morning. I'll meet you at the airport post office. Ask for some stamps; speak French, and apologize for not knowing Italian. I'll be there.'

'All right. I'll make arrangements.'

The tone was peremptory, and I recognized 'Nathalie's' brusque manner. I had been expecting her call. Since Georges had ordered me to trigger the evacuation of the FARL base in Ostia, I had become used to her voice. The night before I had given her a series of messages from her leader. For the past two days I had been virtually immersed in this business. I had seen Georges in prison for the first time on October 29th, and returned to see him again the next day. As far as the press knew, the only famous prisoner

68

being held in Lyons' St Paul Prison was the Nazi war criminal, Klaus Barbie, but I was aware that my client could become as famous as the 'Butcher of Lyons'.

Laurent Gally So you were obeying orders, without question?

J.P.M. Obviously. The Service had asked me to follow instructions from both Georges and his group to the letter, in an attempt to infiltrate and track down all of them. And both 'Nathalie' and Georges considered me a militant, which meant that obedience to them was compulsory.

I immediately informed my superiors of this newest development, and they gave me their approval. Not knowing how long I would be gone, I reserved an open return on the Paris-Rome-Paris flight for the time 'Nathalie' had indicated. And since I did not know where this meeting might lead me I packed my bags with the thought that I might be away from Paris for an indeterminate length of time, in hopes of meeting, if not actually having to follow, other members of the group.

On November 1st, I landed at Fiumicino airport at the time agreed upon and went, as planned, to the post office. In the small, empty room, I asked a bored postal employee for stamps. A young woman entered; she avoided looking at me. She was short, rather plump, and wearing trousers. I registered all this in a flash, without studying her. This was my first mission for the Service outside France, and I was somewhat uneasy about what might happen. What if we were both under surveillance, or were arrested? The Italian authorities must certainly have been following 'Nathalie'.

L.G. Were you 'chaperoned', under surveillance, or under the Service's protection?

J.P.M. I don't know. Later 'they' told me I had been, and described what I had done that day, minute by minute. But at the time I did not notice anyone, which is normal since surveillance was supposed to be discreet so that I would not be 'burned' when dealing with 'Nathalie'. She walked towards me. 'I see you don't speak Italian, Monsieur,' she said, 'may I help you?'

'Thank you,' I said, 'that's very kind of you. I need some stamps for postcards.'

I was trying to act as naturally as possible, but my throat was tight. Still not looking at me, 'Nathalie' translated my request to the postal employee, speaking what seemed to me to be perfect Italian. At the same time she very carefully slipped a bus ticket into my hand and, although we were the only customers in the place, whispered, in French: 'I'll wait for you in the blue bus, in front of the airport.' Then she quickly left the post office.

Picking up my stamps, I made for the exit. The blue bus; which blue bus? There were three or four of them, each going in a different direction. I had a moment of panic: what if I couldn't find her again? What a setback that would be! I studied everyone in the big entrance hall, and even went back inside the terminal to try to spot 'Nathalie'. Suddenly, from afar, I saw her heading towards a bus. I followed her towards it. The destination sign read 'Stazione Termini Roma', Rome's central railway station. The bus was full, but she had saved me a seat beside her.

L.G. What did 'Nathalie' look like?

J.P.M. Black hair and dark eyes. She did not seem to be trying to disguise herself since she wore neither a headscarf nor glasses. I would simply have taken her for a native of Rome. Yet in spite of her casual style, there seemed to me to be something wrong with 'Nathalie's' mouth. It looked as if she might have been operated on for a harelip as a child, and her two front teeth overlapped. I took no real notice of this until a few days later, when the Service showed me photographs of Jacqueline Esber, the FARL terrorist suspected of murdering Israeli diplomat Yacov Barsimantov, in Paris, in early 1982. I immediately recognized 'Nathalie'. The Service told me that Barsimantov's son had chased his father's murderer, and she had turned to face him for a moment. The teenager noticed two things about the woman: she had wide hips (later, the police would elegantly dub her 'Bigass') and her front teeth had a large gap between them, what French country people call 'lucky teeth'.

Hidden by her coat, 'Nathalie's' *derrière* did not seem particularly notable in its dimensions. As for her incisors, which overlapped as if to insist there was no gap between them, a dentist friend later told me that a simple crown can be used to change the general appearance of a person's mouth.

L.G. What did you talk about on the bus?

J.P.M. She immediately wanted to know if I had brought the written messages from Abdallah that I had previously given her over the telephone. She read them quietly, not saying a word, then commented she was surprised Georges had not written them out himself. I did not know what to say but merely assured her that he had insisted on dictating them to me. Then 'Nathalie' searched through her purse and handed me one thousand dollars, in hundred-dollar bills, which was supposed to pay me for my trip and cover the first portion of Abdallah's trial expenses, notably my constant trips between Paris and Lyons. I told myself that she was miserly since my plane ticket alone cost almost half what she was giving me. Obviously, the Service would reimburse me for the trip, but she could not have known that. Of course, it is clear I had not become involved in the affair for the money.

The remainder of the bus ride seemed interminable. I was sweating, and 'Nathalie' did not say a word. She appeared anxious, studying the other passengers and seeming very nervous, no doubt due to my inexperience, which must have been obvious to her. Arriving at the central station, she rose, turned to me and whispered, 'I'll be in touch', then melted into the crowd. I was alone and totally bewildered, my mission ended as soon as it had begun.

It was a holiday in Rome. I wandered through the deserted station, then reserved a seat on the first plane back to Paris. While killing time, I bought a small espresso coffee-maker at a shop inside the station. The Service was still watching me for, long afterwards in Paris, they reproached me for that purchase as an act of carelessness. What if I were being followed by the FARL, my superiors said, wouldn't they be surprised to see me spending 'the cause's' money on an expensive personal item?

L.G. Did you tell them about the meeting right away?

J.P.M. Yes, immediately. I telephoned from the Rome railway station, which was another mistake. I shouldn't have been calling from a public telephone box, since they are all tied into a central switching station where calls can be monitored and where they can trace the number being dialled, even if they cannot listen in to the conversation. And I was dialling a 'secure' line, thus breaking another of the few security rules 'they' had taught me. 'They' would later tell me that the Italian counter-intelligence services had spotted the call and contacted the DSGE in Paris to ask them about it.

So the Service received a request for information regarding a telephone number dialled from the Rome railway station by *Maître* Jean-Paul Mazurier, the terrorists' lawyer! From this I deduced that not only was I being 'covered' by the Service but that I was also under surveillance by their Italian counterparts, who had identified me as the FARL's lawyer. Happily, they did not know that the telephone number in question was a 'secure' one, or they would have immediately become aware of my relationship with the *Piscine*.

On the same night, after returning to Paris, I had to make a fully detailed oral report of my Roman 'stopover'.

L.G. Did you have to wait long before hearing from 'Nathalie' – Jacqueline Esber?

J.P.M. No, because my three trips to meet her – Rome, Geneva and Belgrade – all took place between November 1st and 24th 1984. On my return from Rome I went to see Georges to tell him about my meeting with 'Nathalie'. He asked me to describe the person I had met, as if he feared I had fallen into a trap. Once reassured, he dictated another series of messages to her. This was at the time he still believed his arrest was an error and that he would soon be released. Most of all, as I have said, he seemed to be ordering his comrades to take only 'conservative' measures, meaning that he was instructing that the network, if not their bases, be maintained as it was. He wanted the terrorists to commit no violent acts which might delay his possible release.

I saw Abdallah the day after I returned from Rome, and 'Nathalie' called the following day. The telephone calls continued, keeping time with my journeys between Paris and Lyons.

It was then that the Service decided to install a permanent recording device on my office telephone, one I could turn on and off again at will. Before that the Service had sent two technicians to record my conversations with 'Nathalie'. I even amused myself by recording several telephone conversations that were not exclusively in the interests of the *Piscine*, and recorded, and kept, certain conversations I had with the Service containing unequivocal details of what 'they' expected of me.

Then, one evening in mid-November, 'Nathalie' again asked me to meet her.

'There is a TGV [*Train à Grande Vitesse* – the French high-speed express train] leaving for Geneva in an hour. Be on it; I'll meet you.'

The same laconic style, the same peremptory orders, but I had been instructed to obey without protest. There was just enough time for me to advise my contact and head for the Gare de Lyon. By the time I reached Geneva it was night. She was not on the railway platform and I wandered back and forth, from the buffet to the waiting room, trying to spot 'Nathalie'. No one was there. I waited perhaps a quarter of an hour at most, but it seemed like an eternity. I was on tenterhooks, just as in Rome. I went outside the station, then came back inside again and finally saw her in the entrance hall, dressed almost exactly as she had been at Rome airport. She must have been hiding, trying to spot whether I had been followed, or was being 'chaperoned'.

She greeted me more cordially than during our first meeting. After trying unsuccessfully to find an open restaurant, she dragged me into a cafe. We were the last clients, and before beginning our conversation we ordered some wine. Again, she read Georges' messages, or rather his one message, containing a dozen different points no doubt listed in order of importance.

We discussed one of particular significance: Abdallah was ordering her to mention the word 'operation' if the group was about to enter a more active phase. I could learn no more details and did not know if he actually meant the organization of an attack, but, through a telephone call to me, 'Nathalie' was to inform Georges when the moment was near. Another, minor, point asked 'Nathalie' to give 'the little lawyer' some money. I had questioned Abdallah about his use of that adjective. He answered that my age, and my extremely youthful appearance, justified its use. In revenge, I had changed the part of the message concerning me to read 'a lot of money to the little lawyer', and not merely 'some money'. In later messages Georges would call me 'the little bastard', assuring me that that was a literal translation of an expression of affection in Arabic, a sort of code between him and his comrades. I don't think there was anything fishy about it, since in one of the messages Abdallah dictated to me he had said: 'Raymonda must remain with her little bastard . . .' That was an important reference since it was addressed to someone in his own group, ordering him not to take any personal initiatives, but to await orders in the messages I would be transmitting to them.

'Nathalie' and I had a few drinks, as friends do, or lovers. She inquired about Georges' health, his state of mind, the conditions in the jail where he was being held; all this in perfect French. Then she handed me five hundred dollars. My strategem for augmenting my fee had not impressed her. We parted almost amicably twenty minutes later, she suggesting I find a cheap hotel, and pointing vaguely in the right direction. As always, 'Nathalie' would contact me again by telephone.

L.G. Did you tell the Service immediately?

J.P.M. No, this time I did not repeat the error I had made in Rome. The following morning I telephoned and summed up our very brief meeting. But, as I had in Rome, I again committed several indiscretions by using the 'cause's' money to pay for my luxury hotel room near the station, and for several expensive little purchases such as a portable telephone/clock-radio. At the time I had no idea of the dedicated nature of an agent's life, and did not understand the reasons for the extremely strict rules in effect during the course of a mission.

I returned to Paris the same day and reported in again, once to the Service and once to Georges.

L.G. That reference to the word 'operation'. Did it have any repercussions between your trip to Rome and your trip to Belgrade?

J.P.M. No, I fell back into my usual routine which, by now, meant I was more or less overworking. Abdallah would give me messages, 'Nathalie' would telephone me at night; I was exhausted from the constant running to and fro between Paris and Lyons. The case was still in the hands of the examining magistrate, and I had my other work to attend to. I was at my wit's end. On the other hand, the Service thought it finally had something definite to go on. The FARL were about to go into action, and the *Piscine* would know about it in advance once Georges received the magic word 'operation'. There was a strong possibility they might even be able to control the course of events.

I did not have long to wait. On the morning of Friday 23 November 1984 'Nathalie' telephoned and asked me to buy a one-way plane ticket to Belgrade, Yugoslavia, and to meet her there that same evening. I had a four-hour wait before the plane left Charles de Gaulle airport, but having learned of this new development, the Service forbade me to go. 'They' explained that it was too short notice, that the mission was dangerous (the fact she had ordered me to buy a one-way ticket reinforced that argument), and that 'The Bald One' as they called the in-house financial controller, did not approve. Later I would learn that the Service's refusal was based on the fact that this time I would be going to an Eastern-European country where they could neither cover nor accompany me. I was relatively new to the job and would be on my own, my personal safety at risk. But that made no difference to me since in Rome, as well as Geneva, I had thought I was on my own.

At the very moment I was supposed to be landing in Belgrade, 'Nathalie' telephoned again and was surprised to learn I was still in Paris. After I explained I had been unable to raise the money for the trip, she became insistent, although not pressuring me, saying: 'Come, I need you. I'm ill and must enter the hospital for an operation.'

There it was: the magic word. The Service, who had been waiting for this since Geneva, now excitedly decided I should leave immediately, my safety no longer a factor in the decision-making process.

The next day I was in Belgrade. 'Nathalie' was there, in the airport arrival lounge, and we went up to the second-floor restaurant. I don't know if it was intentional, but all my meetings with 'Nathalie' took place in deserted areas. This one was particularly daunting and I was afraid, but 'Nathalie' seemed perfectly at ease. Was it because she knew me a little better now, or because this meeting was taking place far from the reach of any Western European police? Later, Abdallah would confirm this impression, telling me that his comrades, and Arabs in general, felt quite at home in the Eastern-European countries where they could travel freely and had no problems with visas, or supervision by the authorities.

L.G. The investigations that took place after each terrorist attack revealed that to be a tendency, if not a constant factor. And particularly in Yugoslavia, which was probably the base of operations for the terrorist attack on Rue Marbeuf, in Paris.* And it was again in Yugoslavia that el-Mansuri took the train for Paris, before his arrest.

J.P.M. Correct; but it isn't only Yugoslavia. I can only tell you what I know, personally. When Frédéric Oriach wanted to go to Syria to meet his comrades, Georges told him it would be easier if he went to any Eastern-European capital and waited there for a direct contact. This leads one to believe that in any number of those countries, the FARL had the run of the place.

But in the meantime it was I who was at Belgrade airport, with its cheerful Stalinist architecture. 'Nathalie' opened our meeting by scolding me. First of all, since I was twenty-four hours late, I had made her miss her plane. I repeated that my financial situation did not permit me, credit cards or no, to respond to her invitations as quickly as she might have liked. She then remarked that I should not be among the last passengers to disembark from the plane. I did not understand what she was talking about and attempted to change the subject. Later, Georges would tell me that all terrorists 'find a way' to be among the first passengers leaving a plane, in order to try to spot whether they are being followed. When one is among the last to disembark it is difficult to see who might be following, once one passes through customs.

L.G. Were you still carrying messages for Abdallah?

* This attack, in the summer of 1981, took place outside the office of an Iraqi opposition newspaper, very close to the Champs-Elysées. It left several dead and many wounded, and was attributed to the Venezuelan terrorist Carlos' group, probably under the orders of the Palestinian Abou Nidal.

J.P.M. Of course, as I had during my preceding trips: small pieces of paper covered with short phrases I had already read to 'Nathalie' over the telephone, and which she wanted to verify as to their authenticity. As during my trips to Rome and Geneva, I had left Paris so quickly there had been no time to inform Georges and give him an opportunity to send new messages to his 'confidante', as he had called her in an earlier message.

After scolding me, 'Nathalie' read Georges' messages attentively, then began talking to me about the 'operation'.

'You are to take a room at the Hotel Moscow, in the centre of town,' she said. 'A comrade will contact you there. We call him "the Blond". He'll have details of the operation which you are to transmit to "him". If the comrade can't come to the meeting, I've reserved a seat for you on tomorrow morning's flight to Paris, and you are to meet him at nine tomorrow night, at the cafe downstairs from your office.'

I did not say anything, as I was used to not asking questions. As before, 'Nathalie' referred to Georges as 'him', and did not use his name. I had not known I was to stay in an hotel, and could not understand why she could not give me details about the forthcoming operation herself. The authoritarian tone, dour manner, conciseness, everything about 'Nathalie' suggested she had the soul of a leader, and I realized she must be Georges' right hand, or one of them.

I was filled with a mixture of fear and excitement at the idea of meeting another of the group's cadres, and of learning details of the action they were planning. 'Nathalie' was handing me over to a contact whose responsibility it would be to tell me what I needed to know. Perhaps this was a classic 'cut-out', practised by all revolutionary organizations, since she herself undoubtedly knew all about it. Among her messages to Georges was one saying: 'Those who are near the sea are going to act.'

I must be very precise in describing this episode. The day before I left for Belgrade the mysterious contact had telephoned to cancel our meeting in Paris, leaving a message 'from "Alex" '. Was that mysterious contact 'the Blond?' In any event, the group was trying various ways to reach me so as to let Abdallah know the 'operation' was imminent.

'Nathalie' then handed me an envelope, saying it contained one thousand dollars. When I checked the contents later, one hundred dollars were missing, which seemed strange to me coming from people apparently used to planning their terrorist activities down to the smallest detail. Almost ritually she questioned me about Georges' life in prison, and his state of mind. We had not even ordered a cup of coffee, but sat side by side on the airport bench until she left me, disappearing down a corridor. I immediately read the telexed reservation for my seat on the Paris flight. It was made out in the name 'Mazurien', not 'Mazurier', but I could not tell if that was her mistake, which would have been surprising since I was her official contact with Georges, or the airline's.

I took a taxi to the hotel. It turned out to be a luxury hotel although, when I reached my room, I had to make up my own bed since the sheets were lying folded on the mattress. It must have been around six in the evening and I had nothing to do now but wait for 'the Blond', unable to eat, or go out. Hours passed, hours of reflection, of trying not to think about my growing hunger, my need for sleep, my tension, of listening for the soft sound of footsteps in the corridor. Nothing. Around one in the morning, my nerves stretched to breaking point, I left instructions with the hall porter and went downstairs to the bar. Whisky and Slavic songs took my mind off things for about an hour after which, tense as ever, I went back upstairs to spend the rest of the night in my room, wide awake. 'The Blond' did not come.

Early in the morning I could think of nothing better to do than return to Paris. Curiously, the flight on which 'Nathalie' had booked me stopped in Zurich for four or five hours, which made the trip last a full day. I took advantage of the stopover in Zurich to telephone the Service, give an account of yet another meeting that had not taken place but, most importantly, dictate the messages I was carrying, notably one regarding 'those who are near the sea'. What surprised me most about 'Nathalie's' plan was that she was arranging for me to meet a comrade in the heart of Paris, where before she had always insisted on meeting me outside the borders of France. In fact, she had brought me all the way to Belgrade in order to send me back to Paris! I thought long and hard about that abortive meeting at the hotel, and about the true identity of my contact. Might he be one of 'Nathalie's' superiors? As far as I was concerned, after the Ostia episode, 'those who are near the sea' probably meant terrorists based in Italy.

L.G. This time, had the Service informed its Italian opposite number, even though they hadn't during the Ostia episode? Did the Service try to set a trap at your Paris office?

J.P.M. I'm almost certain our Italian colleagues were informed. As for the arrangements in Paris, they deployed a surveillance team rather than setting a trap, since they had no intention of arresting my 'messenger'. But this was not apparent at the time. The lead-time had been short, and when I entered the almost-deserted cafe the only customers were a couple and a man. They seemed so natural that it never occurred to me they might be working for the Service.

I waited for three-quarters of an hour, in vain. 'The Blond' never appeared. I telephoned my superiors, who ordered me to hang up and go and tell Georges everything that had happened. Georges would later inform me that 'the Blond' had been picked up *en route* to my office, and tortured and killed by Mossad. It's impossible to prove, but many intelligence services from various nations were involved in this affair, not always in full co-ordination. And that's putting it politely! It even occurred to me that if 'the Blond' had arrived early to check out the area, he might have noticed some suspicious comings and goings and left again. He would not necessarily have assumed that I was playing a double game: it would seem normal for Georges' lawyer to be under close surveillance, especially by Mossad.

L.G. Did you ever see Jacqueline Esber again?

J.P.M. No, I never again saw the woman both I and the Service still call 'Nathalie'. After the episode of 'the Blond', all contact with her, even by telephone, ended until early in August 1985, when she again began to give me messages for Georges. Georges would later explain that, through an independent channel of communications, he had ordered his group to break off all contact with me, believing I had been followed to Belgrade, and had committed a number of mistakes which may have cost 'the Blond' his life.

L.G. Still, the message you brought to Abdallah made up for the lack of information from 'the Blond'.

J.P.M. Which, since he had become suspicious of me, was not necessarily in my favour. He knew I was familiar with the phrase 'those who are near the sea', and things had been happening in Italy. First of all, on the day I returned from Belgrade, a man carrying explosives was arrested at Zurich airport.* Although I knew nothing about it at the time, this might have happened while I was waiting in the airport transit lounge. A small item about it appeared in a newspaper, but Georges never brought up the matter, and I cannot prove it had anything to do with my trip.

On the other hand, one or two days after I returned to Paris the Italian police, or, rather, the DIGOS, the Italian equivalent of France's DST, arrested seven or eight Lebanese near Rome on suspicion of preparing a car-bomb to use against the American Embassy, on the Via Veneto. The group claimed they belonged to Islamic Jihad, which to my knowledge is the first time such a claim was made in Europe. Were they 'those who are near the sea'? Abdallah seemed to know those terrorists for, when commenting on their arrest, he said, stonily: 'It doesn't matter, since they didn't find the weapons.' I can't be sure, but those Lebanese were arrested in Ostia, former port of ancient Rome, the same town in which 'Nathalie' had been hiding barely a month earlier. That is the first point.

The second point is that, during that same conversation, Georges assured me the story of the car-bomb was merely a decoy, and that the mysterious group's real aim was to take advantage of the panic that would be generated by the explosion to kidnap the American ambassador. I don't know why he took me into his confidence, especially if he was becoming suspicious of me, nor where he received his information. As far as I can remember, the American diplomat in question was Jewish, and his kidnapping would have drawn Israel into the affair. Also, from having read the judge's case file, and from what Italian colleagues have told me, I

---

* Hani Hussein, a Lebanese national on his way to Rome, carrying two kilograms of explosives.

know that at the time the Lebanese were arrested at their hideout, they had in their possession a blueprint of the embassy, a detailed plan of the car park from which the ambassador's car would be leaving, and details of his daily schedule. According to both the police and the magistrate's dossier, the group was arrested one day before the operation was to take place.

Finally, but this is pure speculation, according to Georges the FARL terrorists make it a point of honour to carry out each of their operations 'perfectly'. And if they are captured, or their plans fail, they claim credit for what they have done in the name of another group whose goals may be similar to their own. At his arrest, Abdallah claimed to be a member of the RMAU. The people arrested in Rome described themselves as members of Islamic Jihad, a plausible claim in Western eyes since that group had already claimed responsibility for the two murderous attacks in Beirut, which caused hundreds of deaths when the drivers of two dynamite-laden cars exploded them in the heart of the French and American peace-keeping contingents.

L.G. What you are saying is that the FARL is, in practice, a terrorist international, and Abdallah is its clandestine leader. Do you believe the Rome 'operation' was the one you were told about in Belgrade?

J.P.M. Everything leads me to that conclusion, but it still remains only a supposition. One must remember that each time the FARL prepared an attack, its organizing cadres would leave the target city the day before. I still wonder where 'Nathalie' was supposed to go, and where she had come from when she was scolding me for having made her miss a flight. Was she leaving fully-prepared and deployed troops behind her? I cannot be sure of any of these hypotheses, but the coincidences are disturbing.

|7| **DAMASCUS**

On 24 March 1985, the French diplomat Gilles Sidney Peyroles was kidnapped in Lebanon. The FARL claimed responsibility for the kidnapping and demanded the freeing of Abdallah in return for Peyroles. A few days later Jean-Paul Mazurier was contacted by the Syrian consulate in Paris with the offer of a Syrian visa – a visa which he had applied for and been refused several months earlier.

The Syrians suggested that he might be able to help Peyroles by visiting Syria. Both Mazurier and the DGSE knew that this was highly improbable, but there were other good reasons for going there. Posing as a tourist, he set off for Damascus with instructions from both the DGSE and Abdallah to try and contact FARL members based at Shtaura, just across the border in Lebanon. It was a mission which turned out to be more difficult – and dangerous – than anyone anticipated.

Jean-Paul Mazurier I was now working almost full time for the DGSE. But the kidnapping of Gilles Sidney Peyroles in Lebanon on 23 March 1985 would change everything. Negotiations for Peyroles' release took place on several levels and, when the FARL quickly claimed responsibility for the kidnapping and indicated that the French government had forty-eight hours to free Abdallah, I found myself for a time in the off-centre eye of the storm. Peyroles, whom they were threatening to execute, was the director of the French cultural centre in the northern Lebanese city of Tripoli. Happily, the FARL did not carry out their threat.

Laurent Gally Were you contacted officially, as Abdallah's lawyer?

J.P.M. I heard nothing from the French side. All negotiations, if we can believe what appeared in the press, were being handled by Algeria. The French government had not forgotten that the passport found on Abdallah at the time of his arrest was an authentic Algerian document, and therefore the Algerian authorities were familiar with the FARL. But on the morning of Wednesday, March 27th, a Syrian diplomat telephoned me at home and said: 'For humanitarian reasons we are granting you the visa for which you applied. Can you be at the consulate at ten tomorrow morning?'

I had met that particular diplomat when, at the end of December 1984, feeling that I was no longer safe in Paris and needed a fall-back position, Georges instructed me to apply for both Lebanese and Syrian visas. I had immediately referred his idea to the Service, who gave me the green light. I first visited the Lebanese consulate in Paris, where my request for a visa was rejected outright: no tourist visas were being granted for Lebanon. A consulate employee looked at me pensively and said: 'If you're trying to commit suicide, there are less expensive ways of going about it. Goodbye, Monsieur.'

I then went to the consulate of Syria, Lebanon's guardian angel. The two countries share a long, common border. There, too, I was received badly. The person behind the counter took my passport, disappeared for a while, then returned and categorically refused my request. When I asked for an explanation, I was led into an office where I reiterated my request to a diplomat, who offered me a cup of coffee. He seemed to be blowing hot and cold, pushing his pawns around a chessboard. He bore a striking resemblance to Omar Sharif, as he said: 'Ever since your president's recent visit to Damascus we no longer intend Syria to have a reputation as a terrorist State, or for protecting terrorists. We know who you are: you are Georges Ibrahim Abdallah's attorney, and you will never be granted a Syrian visa. But my door is always open to you.'

There was nothing I could say. Yet now this same diplomat was just as politely calling me, to hand over the very visa I had given up all hope of ever receiving. I alerted the Service, and they agreed I might go to the next day's meeting, giving me no particular instructions except that I should try to remember everything I could about the consulate, the office, and to study whoever I might see there so as to be able to describe them later, and so on. As if I were the first *Piscine* agent ever to enter the place!

The meeting was extremely cordial. The diplomat was not alone this time, but introduced me to one of his colleagues, evidently a person of some authority.

'We are granting you a visa so that you may do something for Peyroles . . .'

'That's very nice of you,' I said, 'but I'm not involved in that affair. I want a tourist visa; I'm not going on a diplomatic mission.'

I played the innocent, as the Service had told me to do, and quite clearly they weren't buying it, even though they went through the motions. Then, even more incredibly, they said:

'If you could also find some way to do something for Messrs Carton and Fontaine* . . . Do come to see us when you return; we receive very little news about what's going on there . . . When you are in Syria you will have the advantage of certain direct, or even indirect, assistance . . .'

I continued my childish denials, insisting I was merely travelling as a tourist. The men suggested to me, unofficially, that the FARL might not only be responsible for kidnapping Peyroles but also for holding the other two French diplomats hostage. That kidnapping was officially being claimed by the Islamic Jihad organization in Beirut. Without asking for my approval the Syrians then tele-phoned the head of Syrian Airlines in Paris to reserve a seat for me on the Paris-Frankfurt-Damascus flight. I was to be charged the same price as that reserved for Syrian citizens! I felt like a pawn that they could move around however they liked.

L.G. Do you actually believe this all sounds plausible, you allowing yourself to be manipulated, on orders? Or are you fabricating these memories?

* Marcel Carton and Marcel Fontaine – French diplomats kidnapped in Beirut on 22 March 1985.

J.P.M. I can only repeat what I've said. It's too late now, and I've gone too far, to try to embroider the story. Time was short when I left the Syrian consulate. I telephoned the Service, which confirmed that I was to leave immediately, and released the dollars I would need before going to the airline office.

It was extremely important that we test Georges' reaction to the Syrian proposal, so I visited the Santé Prison that afternoon to ask his permission to leave. Holding his head in his hands, he questioned his own reading of the situation and tried to decide whether or not I should go. According to Georges, there was a handwritten note, in Arabic, on the Syrian visa that might prove very troublesome upon my arrival in Damascus. In his opinion the Syrians were obviously setting a trap for me, but he could not divine what was behind this precipitous journey. At last, he wrote a long letter that I was to give to his comrades, but he did not give me the exact address or the name of the people I was to contact. I was to telephone *As Safir*, the Lebanese left-wing newspaper, and tell someone in the editorial department that I was Abdallah's lawyer, and that I had just arrived in Syria.

The meeting went so quickly that I didn't think to ask Georges about the Syrians' reference to Carton and Fontaine, the two diplomats being held hostage. I did not even bring up the 'suggestion' concerning Peyroles, as I feared Georges might forbid me to go.

He had mentioned Peyroles during my preceding visit, slipping in a word or two as if it did not concern him directly. 'The man's an agent. They've all been spotted a long time ago.' He said it with such scorn I hadn't dared press the issue. His disdain brutally underlined my own awkward situation, and I quickly cut the meeting short. He did not mention the ultimatum his group had issued regarding his own release. Just before I arrived he had had a visit from *Maître* Jacques Vergès, but I do not know if he discussed the matter with his other defence lawyer . . .

L.G. Did Abdallah ever speak about the series of kidnappings that had occurred in Lebanon? Was he in favour of that sort of action, in principle?

J.P.M. He never referred to any particular kidnapping, apart from his comment on Peyroles' alleged duties there, for the good reason that he disapproved of taking hostages. He considered himself as being held hostage in France. With hindsight, it seems to me that Georges allowed me to go to Syria so that I might reach his comrades and remind them there was no question simply of exchanging Peyroles for himself without first making sure that Paris would not expel him from France, back to Beirut. The Lebanese Phalange would have murdered him immediately.

L.G. In your opinion, what was the Syrians' aim in granting you the visa?

J.P.M. It was obvious I was being manipulated by the Syrians. Granting Abdallah's lawyer a visa was, no doubt, only one of their numerous goodwill gestures during the Peyroles affair, which had embarrassed them considerably. Everyone knew their troops controlled the area in which he had been kidnapped, if not the immediate zone where he was being held hostage.

As for their motives in talking to me about Peyroles, Carton and Fontaine, it was up to the Service to judge them. Did they suspect me of working for the *Piscine*? Not necessarily: I had requested the visa some three months earlier, before the Peyroles affair. The fact that I was agreeing to go to Syria at that critical moment, and within twenty-four hours of receiving a visa, should have made me hesitate, but I was too excited, as was the Service. And then, perhaps the Syrians knew Abdallah trusted me, and that I would be carrying a message, if only an oral one, from him to his troops. Whether it was a message of moderation, which would suit them, or a message to stand firm, they would have the means to neutralize me, since I would be in their hands.

L.G. What was the DGSE analysis of your meeting at the consulate?

J.P.M. That evening I handed over Abdallah's letter to the Service for translation and decoding, so that they might analyze his intentions. It was not until the next day, only a few hours before my plane was to leave, that my superiors came to fetch me, to talk over what was behind this trip to Damascus. Like Abdallah, they were extremely worried something terrible might happen to me there. So they advised me, as soon as I arrived, to telephone a 'secure' number they were setting up for the occasion. They were still committed to the official story that this was strictly a holiday trip. To that effect, they suggested I buy a camera! They were surprised at the Syrians' suggestions regarding Carton and Fontaine, but did not comment on them. Nor did they discuss Peyroles, as there was absolutely no question of my doing anything to help regain his freedom. My sole assignment was to find some way to reach Shtaura, in Lebanon, contact members of the FARL there and bring back as much information about them as I could.* I was aware of being nothing but a pawn, and that people were manipulating me while telling me as little as possible.

Feeling like a front-line soldier in a military operation I left for Syria. Later, one of my contacts would say: 'We were all behind you.'

L.G. It's true. Throughout this entire affair you give the impression of acting like a soldier under fire, following orders even though you knew nothing of the battle plan, neither your own side's, nor the enemy's.

J.P.M. That is exactly the way it was. I was a 'Black Agent'. I had been in the Service only a few months, had received no training, but those were the rules of the game and I had accepted them. On this assignment I was in a hurry to reach Damascus, no matter what the consequences might be, and find the FARL who, through my contacts with Abdallah and my abortive meetings with 'Nathalie', had begun to take on mythological proportions in my mind. For the first time I had the feeling I would truly be in the front line even if, in the Service's eyes, my meetings with Abdallah already counted as such. We, the Service and I, had become accustomed to dealing with the chief link in the chain; now we wanted to roll up the entire network. Personally, I thought the FARL could only be more dangerous deprived of their leader. But I had no illusions about my playing a role in freeing Peyroles.

L.G. Were your fears confirmed once you arrived in Damascus?

J.P.M. I felt as if I was in enemy territory the moment I took my

* When Abdallah suggested that Mazurier go to Lebanon, at the end of 1984, he had told him to ask the help of his group in the town of Shtaura.

seat in the aeroplane. There was nothing particularly ominous, except for the presence of the head of Syrian Airlines in Paris, the very man the diplomats had telephoned. I was distracted from my worries by the pilot putting the plane into a nose-dive so the passengers might admire the mountains of Crete. Each time the plane banked it went into such a tight turn that the centrifugal force tore one of the seats loose. As a passenger, I hardly felt any better myself.

When we arrived in Damascus I had no difficulties going through customs and the police check. A taxi driver picked me up – I would see him again later – and even though I asked him, in English, which he understood perfectly, to take me to an inexpensive hotel, he drove me to the luxury Chams Hotel. I found myself in an anonymous hotel room, watching an adventure film, in French, on television. Most of the people in the hotel spoke French, including the young Tunisian waiter who claimed he had studied engineering in Moscow.

I did not telephone the 'secure' number the Service had set up, to assure them all was well, as ordered. I thought such a telephone call might draw attention to me, but this turned out to be a grave error since I put Paris on a state of alert from the very start of the mission.

From my hotel room I telephoned *As Safir*, the Lebanese newspaper Abdallah had given me as a contact. I don't know why, but from Damascus one could call Lebanon only between midnight and six in the morning. Someone, probably a journalist, answered the telephone, and I introduced myself, describing who I was. He told me he would send the paper's leading reporter to see me the next day.

So I sat down to wait, in vain, for the whole of the next day as well as the day after. I had arrived on March 29th. It was now the 31st and I was eager to do something, even if the journalist had stood me up. I questioned everyone, the waiters as well as the hotel's French manager, as to the simplest way to cross the Lebanese border, frankly admitting I didn't have a visa.

L.G. Isn't that even more obvious: a tourist who never leaves his hotel, then politely asks how to make a trip that is clearly prohibited?

J.P.M. Not necessarily. I was a tourist, and I had heard that Lebanon was a magnificent country, we were only a forty-five-minute taxi ride away from Shtaura, the nearest Lebanese town, and the manager explained that numerous tourists made the day trip from Damascus to Shtaura and back again, leaving their passports at the border when they entered Lebanon and picking them up again on their return.

Still, the manager was being very careful. He thought it sheer folly for a Frenchman to go to Lebanon without a visa, especially since Peyroles was still being held hostage. He advised me to first go to Amman, the Jordanian capital, which is only two or three hours away by taxi, where I could apply for a visa at the Lebanese consulate. There was no Lebanese consulate in Damascus, as if the Syrians did not consider their neighbours independent, but rather as 'brothers' who had, unhappily, been separated from them by history.

I asked the hotel's Syrian assistant manager to order a taxi to pick me up early the next morning. Then I went to the Italian restaurant in the hotel, which has three separate restaurants: Chinese, international and Italian. I ordered a meal I had eaten there before, lasagna and wine. Around five o'clock, in the middle of the meal, I suddenly became violently ill. Two waiters had to carry me, half-conscious, to my room. When I woke again it was dark; my bedside clock read six. I dressed hastily, worried that the taxi I had ordered would not wait for me. Going down to the lobby I searched, in vain, for the taxi. While waiting for it to arrive I asked for my bill, but it was payable only in dollars and I had nothing but Syrian money. The dollars I had brought with me from Paris had been stolen during the night, I suppose. Very nervous, but not wanting to make a scene, I asked if I might change some money.

'Turn to the right as you leave the hotel, Monsieur; you will see a small jewellery store. They will change money for you.'

Automatically I walked out of the hotel, only to discover that the street was filled with people and that all the neon lights were on. At six in the morning? Suddenly it became clear to me: it was six in the evening, not six in the morning. Panicked, I returned to the lobby. The calendar on the concierge's desk read, Monday, April

1st. The April Fool's joke was turning sour. I had 'slept' for a whole twenty-five hours! My stomach cramps and nausea were straight out of a spy novel. I had been drugged, which had given 'them' time to neutralize me and search my luggage . . . and find the letter Georges had sent to his people. The next day, in Amman, I would learn that while I 'slept', Peyroles had been released.

I was frightened, but determined to carry out my mission, no matter what the cost. I ordered a taxi to pick me up at four in the morning, then went to dine . . . in the same Italian restaurant, even ordering the same pasta and wine. It was not even a gesture of defiance: the wine, or the water, might have been drugged no matter which restaurant I chose. But nothing else happened, and the next day the taxi was there on time.

L.G. Did your mission still have any meaning, after that very revealing 'delay'?

J.P.M. At the time I did not know Peyroles had been released, but I was on a different mission, and had no intention of coming back empty-handed. I realized I was under constant surveillance, but I wanted to act step by step, confronting any obstacles that might arise one at a time.

My taxi driver spoke little English and was extremely dour. The trip to Amman took hours, the taxi driving past several military roadblocks without stopping, even though private vehicles were being searched. We stopped for the usual customs formalities. Since it was still dark I couldn't even see the landscape. Entering Amman I was struck by the number and size of the gigantic pictures of King Hussein hanging at every street corner.

I did not stay long in Amman. The Lebanese consulate refused my request for a visa, saying I should have applied for it in Paris, as all French citizens were supposed to! I didn't press the matter: the taxi driver assured me that, with enough *baksheesh*, I could easily cross the Syrian-Lebanese border.

So we returned directly to Damascus, where the taxi driver took the road to Shtaura. The trip seemed interminable as the driver stopped a dozen times to tell his friends he was going to Lebanon, and ask if they wanted him to bring back food or other goods, since prices were much cheaper there than in Syria. I was bored to death by each delay, every detour, but I was dependent on the driver's good will and was also reassured by those stops. If he was taking orders, we would surely be able to enter Lebanon easily, as he had said. I frequently checked the road behind us. We were not being openly followed, although that didn't mean a thing as all that is needed is a telephone.

After filling out the usual forms, we moved past Syrian customs and the border police, then Lebanese customs. But the Lebanese police stopped us. I watched as my driver spoke to them in Arabic, holding out bundles of Syrian pounds. The uniformed subordinate seemed uninterested, which greatly surprised my driver. The border police officer didn't say a word to me, but merely glanced at me before inspecting my passport. He must have had strict orders.

I was determined to cross the border. Coming out of the police station I tried to negotiate with the other policemen there. Nonchalantly, they aimed their Kalashnikovs at me. They could not have been more than sixteen or seventeen years old. I even offered to leave my passport with them. Again, a stubborn refusal. Other cars were driving past me.

Suddenly a black sedan carrying four very quiet, very elegantly dressed men stopped beside me. One of the passengers rolled down his window and said: 'Where are you going, Monsieur? May I help you?'

I hesitated, scrutinizing their faces before committing myself.

'I'm going to Shtaura.'

'That's fine; we're going there too.'

In fact, we were barely ten minutes from Shtaura. I had to tell him I had no visa.

'That doesn't matter. Get in.' I could sense that he meant it and, in a flash, remembered the Syrian diplomat handing me my visa and saying: 'You'll have certain direct, or indirect, assistance . . .' But I was afraid. Their faces were stern, and suddenly the car looked like a coffin.

'Thank you, that's very kind of you, but I have a taxi. My driver will take me.'

'You're sure you don't want to come with us?' one of the men insisted. Again, I refused. He stared at me, then rolled up his window, and the black car moved away.

I felt as if, perhaps, I had let a chance slip by that would never come again but, at the same time, I was not sorry. The car might have taken me into I don't know what trap, or to my death. But I was still stuck at the border, facing the impassive and disquieting border police. My gallant cab driver suggested I did not press the matter, but return to Damascus.

With no money left, I resigned myself to one last try. Scribbling a short note, I told the cab driver to give it to the pastry shop owner in Shtaura, of whom Abdallah had spoken, although he had not told me the man's name. The message was brief: 'I'm "the" Frenchman, and I'm stuck at the border. Come and get me.' I was aware how rash this was, and how small my chances of success, but I had no other choice and, realizing how obvious I appeared, waited inside the police station for my driver to return. Happily, I do not understand Arabic and so was spared understanding any conversations that might have made me blanch.

I supposed I would have to wait half an hour, or forty-five minutes at the most, but it was almost four hours before my taxi returned, packed to its roof with merchandise. At least the driver hadn't wasted his time. We had left Damascus at four in the morning. It was now around nine-thirty at night. Calmly, my driver informed me he had not been able to find the pastry cook at Shtaura, that he was sorry, but that we would now have to return to Damascus. I felt miserable, and absolutely helpless.

So I returned to the Chams Hotel, which I had hated ever since being poisoned, and had expected never to see again. Despite my sorry financial state I asked the driver to make the trip to Shtaura again the next day, in order to try to reach the 'comrades' through the pastry shop owner. Ironically, the desk clerk gave me the same room I had left at daybreak. I had no money to pay the bill.

Entering the room, I was greeted by another surprise: the telephone had been ripped from the wall and now lay between the twin beds, its wires exposed. I had no doubt I'd been followed wherever I went, but no longer had the strength to wonder why the Syrians would want to wreck a telephone equipped with bugging devices that must have cost them a fortune. Still unable to work it out, I fell asleep.

The next day, Wednesday, I waited for my taxi driver to appear at around noon. Noon passed. I was broke, and was growing more and more anxious. Seating myself in the lobby, I waited there until nine in the evening. Finally, the hotel manager telephoned the taxi service: not wanting to waste money on petrol, the driver had stayed at home. Leaving my lawyer's identity card as security (it is still there) I moved to the French-owned Méridien Hotel, where I could have the bill paid by telex from Paris.

The next day I increased my efforts towards crossing the border, and telephoned my family in Paris to bail me out of the financial mess in which I now found myself. It took hours, but by nightfall I was able to reserve a taxi to take me to Shtaura on Friday morning. The next morning, the same driver who had brought me to Damascus from the airport was there. The Syrian capital was certainly a small world. The man seemed happy enough to see me and promised he would take me wherever I wanted to go, no matter what the difficulties. But despite my driver's efforts, the Lebanese border guards were no more willing to allow me to cross than before.

Rather that give up and return to Damascus, I asked the driver to stop while I tried to find another way across. There were innumerable Syrian military trucks in the area. One stopped and, in an approximation of English, a young soldier no older than sixteen or seventeen asked me what I was doing there. Finally, after some cash changed hands, he offered to take me into Shtaura. I handed him some three hundred Syrian pounds, not a large sum to me but certainly a goodly amount to him, and the soldiers helped me up into the truck. The truck turned on to a road running parallel to the main highway and separated from it by a high chainlink fence. This road was reserved for military convoys headed for Lebanon, and bypassed the border inspection.

Uneasy at having entrusted my safety to the goodwill of those adolescents, I lay flat on my belly at the back of the truck. The soldiers were seated in two rows, their feet in my face, their Kalashnikovs between their knees. If only someone had been there to snap that picture! A short while later the truck stopped and the soldiers threw me off. We were less than two hundred metres from the border. I could see the guard post in the distance. But the police had spotted me too. They ran towards me, their automatic weapons pointing in my direction. But still I refused to give up. They threatened me, the tone of their voices leaving no doubt as to what they were saying until, finally, the police commandant himself came for me, urging me towards his office with blows from his swagger-stick.

My humiliation was total. I was enraged: I had been swindled and ridiculed. Again the officer questioned me, demanding to know the name of the friends I wanted to see so urgently, in Shtaura. 'Georges,' I mumbled. He repeated the word, one hand waving in the air, then showed me the register in which the name of everyone crossing the border, in either direction, was noted.

'Read this,' he said. 'You're the only foreigner on the list. You're getting famous around here. Now, go back to Damascus.'

I tried to protest one last time, saying that I was broke, and counting on my friends in Shtaura for money. In vain. Faced with my relentless insistence, the officer held his head in his hands and, no doubt wondering what arguments other than force would be necessary, herded me back toward my still-waiting taxi. As we drove back toward the city my driver tried to console me, saying: 'I'm sorry, Monsieur. I'm sorry for you . . .'

Defeated, and filled with rage, I stared out at the arid landscape. Lebanon, the forbidden land, had seemed verdant to me, with its eternally snow-capped mountains in the distance and its lush vegetation. Reaching Damascus in the middle of the afternoon, I took refuge in one of the Méridien's lounges and brooded on my failure. My plane was scheduled to leave the following afternoon. I still had the morning in which to try again.

But next morning, weary and sick as a dog from having been poisoned, I gave up. Reluctant to return to Paris carrying the weight of my failure, I dragged myself on to the Syrian Airlines plane, and settled down into my seat. The pilot welcomed everyone aboard and the aeroplane doors were already closed, when a hostess announced, 'Monsieur Mazurier is wanted on the flight deck.'

Surprised, I made for the front of the plane. At that moment the door opened again, and I felt myself being pushed out. Four men were staring at me across the width of the passenger bridge, which was still extended.

'Monsieur, you did not pay the bill for your last night's stay at the Chams Hotel.'

It was a lie, but I had no proof. After receiving the money telexed from Paris to the Méridien Hotel, I had returned to the Chams to pay my bill, but had forgotten to ask for a receipt. Dumbfounded at this latest in my series of misadventures, I attempted to argue. The plane was about to leave. I handed them the last of my dollars: they seemed disappointed. They had probably thought I had no money, which would have permitted them to detain me in Damascus.

L.G. Listening to your story, one has the impression that the Syrians constantly tried to humiliate you. Was there any way they could have known you were an agent, and on a mission?

J.P.M. I don't know. I committed many, sometimes grave, errors on that trip but I can make no comments about them since they have to do with security matters. What is certain is that I was behaving like an irresponsible idiot, making a spectacle of myself, but I truly had no choice.

On my return my superiors greeted me coldly. One of them even said, 'You're starting to become dangerous,' which gave me chills down my spine. They still tease me about my 'Syrian Campaign', as if it were Napoleon's retreat from Moscow. I was reprimanded several times, and the Service reportedly received several urgent cables demanding an explanation about 'that crazy person you sent us'. Later, I would hear contradictory stories. First, that I had almost undermined Peyroles' release, although how I did was never explained to me; and second, an opinion from my boss, 'Actually, it's not a bad thing that you failed in your mission. If you'd carried it off, you'd probably have been killed.'

L.G. Are such failures usual among agents in the field?

J.P.M. No. It's a profession where failure is not allowed. When I returned, I was so ill that 'they' ordered me to take a holiday. As far as I was concerned, six weeks with no contact was holiday in itself. I also did not see Abdallah during that time. Upon my return I had told him about the trip and he reproached himself for having told me to go. 'It's my fault,' he said, 'I should never have let you leave.'

The Service was keeping me on, since I was still Georges' lawyer, but I was so desperate I even considered resigning from the bar. I went so far as to confess my faults of omission to the bar council, but nothing came of it.

L.G. Once you were back in Paris you must have heard of the developments in the Peyroles affair, and that Abdallah would not be released, since he had become known to the public when the DST discovered the FARL arsenal in a Paris apartment.

J.P.M. Yes, but don't forget I only went to see Georges on that one occasion, that I was in terrible physical shape, and that the discovery of the arsenal became known while I was in Damascus. Of course, Abdallah was now a public figure, the press was describing him as being the number-one terrorist, but at the time he said nothing to me about the DST raid.

But the consequences of that announcement would be incalculable. Instead of being released, Georges found himself with an extended lease on his prison cell. The discovery of the weapons cache provided a new reason to open a second judicial inquiry against him, this time in Paris. And that dossier would lead him to be tried in the Assizes Court for complicity in three terrorist attacks for which the FARL had claimed responsibility in 1982.* I did not represent him in that case since he himself thought it to be of secondary importance. And the full scope of its seriousness would not become apparent until 1986, when he was tried and sentenced in Lyons.

As for the Rue Lacroix weapons cache: was that the 'strategic material' I had been assigned to move? It's possible, even though I doubt it, since the nature and quantity of the weapons was similar,

---

* The FARL arsenal was discovered in an apartment rented by Abdallah and Jacqueline Esber at 18 Rue Lacroix, Paris. A Czechoslovakian-made CZ70 automatic found there was, according to ballistics experts, the weapon used in the murders of Lieutenant-Colonel Charles Ray, Military Attaché at the American Embassy in Paris, in January 1982, and Yacov Barsimantov in April 1982.

according to what 'Alex' told me at the time. But there is no way of knowing if either side is telling the truth.

The important thing in the Syrian episode is that during the Peyroles affair, the *Piscine* somehow managed to distance itself from the Abdallah case, unlike the DST, whose motives still give me pause for thought. Did someone deliberately try to impede Georges' release? Had the government made any promises? Beyond the mere facts of the judicial process, Abdallah's detention had now become a political case, both domestically and at international level.

|8| **ROME AND TRIESTE**

After his disastrous Syrian mission, Jean-Paul Mazurier needed time to recover from the effects of the poisoning. But by mid-May he was back at work again, and although he was no longer acting as Abdallah's messenger, he was still his lawyer. El-Mansuri, whom Mazurier had visited in Trieste, and another FARL member, Joséphine Abdo Sarkis, had just been tried in Italy for the transportation of explosives and had been given long sentences. Abdallah asked Mazurier to go to Italy and organize their appeals. When Mazurier arrived in Italy he learned that the two faced further charges of assassination and other terrorist activities. They were to be tried in Rome, later that summer.

Jean-Paul Mazurier My return from Damascus was a catastrophe. My morale had hit rock bottom and I was not in much better shape physically. I never did learn if I had been drugged or poisoned at the Chams Hotel, for the lab tests made a week after my return to Paris disclosed nothing. But there were side-effects. My sight was affected: for the next two months my eyes ran constantly, and I lost forty per cent of the vision in my right eye. My vision would slowly return over the next eighteen months. Meanwhile, I was blind as a bat in more ways than one, because, as the Service had ordered me to back off and take a holiday, I was no longer working on the Abdallah case for them.

There was no more for me to do as Georges' 'messenger', but as a lawyer I was soon back in the saddle again. In mid-May 1985, my handler in the Service informed me that Mansuri, the 'lion cub' I had visited in Trieste, and a Lebanese woman named Joséphine Abdo Sarkis, had just been sentenced to sixteen and fifteen years in prison, respectively, by the Trieste court.

Laurent Gally Did you know Abdo? And why hadn't you defended Mansuri?

J.P.M. Abdo was arrested in December 1984, while in transit at Rome's Fiumicino airport. I don't know precisely what evidence the Italians had against her, but the French media reported that 'Barsimantov's murderer' had been arrested in Rome. During one of my visits to Lyons, just prior to Georges being transferred to Paris's Santé Prison, I mentioned this to him. He did not say a word, and did not ask me to go and see her as he had for Mansuri, nor did he ask me to represent her. For my part, I had no idea Abdo was 'the Englishwoman' Georges had mentioned in an early message. Georges' behaviour at the time was a reflection of his suspicions about me.

There is another possibility. Mansuri had been assigned an Italian public defender, and Abdo had chosen a Rome lawyer, Edmundo Zappacosta, whom Georges mockingly called 'El Libertador'. Knowledgeable in the law, Georges believed his friends to be in no particular danger. Of course, Mansuri was charged with transporting explosives, a crime that, based on recent precedent-setting cases, might bring him a three- or four-year prison term if the indictment was merely for transporting, and it was not proved that he intended to use them within the country. Abdo was charged with complicity in the transportation of explosives. The indictment was based on her links with Georges, who had rented an apartment for her in Spain, and another in Ostia.

But the Trieste trial had not gone well. The trial date was not announced to the press, which was curious if the government's intention was to underline the struggle-against-terrorism aspects of it. Mansuri was not given an interpreter even though he could barely speak Italian. And so on. The Italian penal code provides for a maximum fifteen-year prison term for transporting explosives, and Abdo, like Mansuri, received the maximum sentence. Another year was added to Mansuri's sentence for his use of a forged Moroccan passport. Why were the sentences so heavy? Studying the case files and court transcripts later, I saw that the judges had decided the case based on a document, written in Italian, and entered into evidence as the purported transcript of Georges' interrogation when he was being held in custody in Lyons. He had described himself as the head of the FARL and, to make things worse, reportedly revealed his true identity, Georges Ibrahim Abdallah, during the course of the first questioning session, admitting he had ordered Mansuri to bring the explosives to Rome to be used in bombings there.

L.G. That document was not a translation of one of the transcripts from the French case file?

J.P.M. Obviously not. In the course of the early questioning sessions in Lyons, not only had Mansuri never been mentioned, but Abdallah never claimed to be the head of the FARL, a confession officials of the French justice system had tried, in vain, to obtain, since he never mentioned any group except the RMAU. Naturally, the police recognized the many similarities between the aims of the RMAU and the FARL, but those were merely suspicions, which the Trieste document had now transformed into certainties. And then there is the matter of Abdallah's true identity, which I defy anyone to find anywhere in the French case file. Georges had always refused to sign his name to the transcripts, and was still writing to me under the name Saadi Abdelkader.

How had the Italian translation of a document that would prove so damaging to Mansuri come into existence? One theory is that this forgery, for that is what it is, as I later told several Italian examining magistrates, was the work of the Italian DIGOS. They could not have learned anything from Mansuri, for the 'lion cub', who wasn't even sixteen years old at the time, was so stubbornly keeping his mouth shut that a physician was called in to try to determine if he was mute! A second possibility is that the forged translation was the work of the French. The document was entered as evidence in the Trieste trial (and, later, in Rome, where it would figure at every step in the judicial procedure) as being the result of an international rogatory commission, which itself was a response to the Italian court's request to France for information about the affair.

On which side of the Alps was the forgery committed? Was it created before, or during, the translation of the original document into Italian? Whichever it was, there was certainly police malfeasance, while the Trieste magistrates were content to allow themselves to be duped. In fact, their decision had an impact on almost every FARL leader the police uncovered. Jacqueline Esber was tried, by default, for conspiracy to transport explosives, but was acquitted for lack of proof. On the other hand, Daher Ferial, another FARL militant, whom the press claimed was Georges' Parisian 'fiancée', was sentenced *in absentia* to fifteen years in prison, like Abdo, for the same crime, after investigators established she was on the train with Mansuri.

L.G. You have made a serious accusation. Forged documents, if used in a trial, whether they are the work of the police or of the prosecution, render their authors liable to a criminal charge of falsification of public documents.

J.P.M. I'm aware of that, but I have already gone public with the problem, both when I was pleading Abdo and Mansuri's case and afterwards, when I represented Abdallah at his trial in Lyons. I am repeating it here, for I am a lawyer and I think it dangerous for a democracy to have to manipulate evidence in order to arrive at its ends. Even if it seems to be primarily of judicial interest, I am describing this matter in detail because I think it is an exemplary case. It reminds me of the Orson Welles film, *Touch of Evil*, in which Welles played a police officer who invented evidence against people he knew were guilty, but whom he could not arrest any other way. I firmly believe these methods must only be used in movies, or detective novels. Democratic countries must fight terrorism without themselves breaking the law, or they undermine their very being.

L.G. How did Georges react to those guilty verdicts?

J.P.M. On orders from the Service I went back to see him, as I had only visited him once since my return from Damascus. I reappeared at a crucial moment. The guilty verdicts were going to bring me back into the action, since a lawyer was needed to sort out this Italian affair. Georges received me very warmly, and after greeting me asked me to go to Italy to see Abdo and Mansuri, and organize their appeal trials. The severity of the sentences had stunned him.

I went to see Abdo twice, in July and September of 1985, but only Abdo, since the prosecutor in Trieste would still remember my first visit there. I knew nothing about the young woman. Georges asked me to kiss her and whisper: 'I am your brother.' Georges called Abdo 'the Englishwoman' in his messages because she spoke fluent English, but not French.

Joséphine Abdo was being held in Rebibia, a maximum-security prison on the outskirts of Rome that also housed a number of members of the Red Brigades. She had been placed in isolation. The Italian authorities had reacted almost hysterically to the alleged FARL activities, since immediately after the sentencing in Trieste a bomb explosion killed three people at the Alitalia office in Frankfurt, Germany. Responsibility for that attack was claimed, in a telephone call, in the name of the Arab Revolutionary Movement, which one can easily mistake for the RMAU, the group Georges had claimed to belong to when first arrested.

I obtained a pass for one visit, as I had with Mansuri. When Abdo entered the visitors' room, I rushed to her, took her in my arms, and whispered the password. Abdo seemed extremely wary of me, and I feared she would turn around and go back to her cell rather than speak to me. After reading a letter from Georges, which I managed to slip into her hand, she explained her wariness by saying that, at first glance, she had taken me for a secret agent who had come to kill her!

That paranoia was not unjustified. Abdo told me that over the past two days she had been visited by two men she judged to be Mossad agents. They had tried to question her, then had threatened to have her extradited to Israel. Of course, it was impossible to verify her statements. She also described seeing some very excited French policemen who had arrived after her arrest, evidently certain they at last had their hands on the murderer of Israeli diplomat Yacov Barsimantov (which might also explain the sudden appearance of Mossad agents) and who must have been extremely disappointed when she did not match the physical description sent by the criminal investigations department. Josephine had also been confronted, in vain, with American diplomat Christian Chapman, who had been the victim of a FARL assassination attempt in Paris, in late 1981, but he was unable to identify her as one of his attackers. In a message sent in November 1984, Georges himself had insisted that Abdo 'had nothing to do with all that'.

Joséphine Abdo was twenty-seven years old, short, rather thin and had a very sweet face. Happy by nature, she even laughed about her imprisonment. She had black, wavy, shoulder-length hair and dark, expressive eyes. She radiated a simple, extremely feminine charm, quite the opposite of Jacqueline Esber, for example. Abdo was visibly pure and innocent: she seemed to believe totally in her political ideas.

I was immediately able to ask her to name me as her lawyer, and she explained her legal situation to me, which turned out to be more serious than I had imagined. Besides the matter brought to trial in Trieste, the Italians had also indicted her for the assassination of the American general Leamon Hunt, former commander of the Multinational Force in the Sinai, which had taken place in Rome in February 1984.* She had also been indicted on the general charge of 'belonging to an armed band', as well as for 'all the attacks and carnage', as I translated it, that had occurred in Italy over the last two years and had not been cleared up.

L.G. The Italian authorities were piling up the charges against her. But the Rome government was also taking a political risk, the Frankfurt bombing proves that. FARL might have decided to concentrate on Italy as their primary theatre of operations.

J.P.M. Absolutely. I even thought that the business of the forged documents, which had led to the guilty verdicts at Trieste, might have been a 'poisoned' present from the French police to their Italian colleagues. What was certain was that if members of the FARL were still in Europe, they would not just sit back and allow their comrades to be sentenced to long terms in prison. We did not have long to wait. There was a murderous 'warning attack'

---

* Three groups claimed responsibility for the assassination, which took place on 15 February 1984, including both the FARL and the Italian Red Brigades.

at the Café de Paris, on Rome's Via Veneto, just before Abdo and Mansuri were to go on trial again. No doubt the Italians also received warnings sent from Beirut, as the French were receiving threats regarding Abdallah.

I cannot exclude the idea that the FARL might have come to suspect the French, rather than the Italians, of having forged the documents since there were no attacks in Italy throughout 1986, even though Abdo and Mansuri were still in jail there. But the bomb explosion at the Pont-Show Gallery, on Paris's Champs-Elysées, on 20 March 1986, came only ten days after the Court of Appeals confirmed the sentence handed down in Trieste. Those claiming responsibility for the bombing demanded, for the first time in France, Abdo and Mansuri's release. It was as if rather than take on the Italian government, the FARL had gone back to the origins of the affair.

L.G. Once you had established contact with Abdo, did you regularly act as a messenger between her and Abdallah? And were you of any use to the *Piscine* in your role as a lawyer before the Rome trial?

J.P.M. I carried messages in both directions between Abdo and Abdallah, but there weren't many since I only saw Joséphine twice before the trial opened. I believe the information she entrusted to me, uncoded and written in Arabic, was of some importance. Slipping the letters into my hand, she would say: 'Go, and don't get caught, because if you are we will both have to serve another fifteen years.'

The risks I was taking were obvious. We were under constant surveillance by three extremely wary female guards. I was never physically searched, but my Italian colleagues informed me that a number of lawyers had been caught, and received long sentences for, for example, helping their Red Brigades clients, even in humanitarian matters. And a Rome lawyer had just committed suicide when the police, who were coming to arrest him, rang his doorbell.

The Service translated the letters I was carrying to Georges, but did not keep me abreast of what resulted from them. During this period I completely regained the FARL's trust, I believe, culminating with my obtaining Abdo and Mansuri's acquittal at the Rome trial, as well as that of Jacqueline Esber and Daher Ferial, who were again being tried *in absentia*.

L.G. Describe the trial proceedings.

J.P.M. The setting was dismal. For security reasons, the hearing was held inside Rebibia Prison, in a room that had already been used for several Red Brigades trials. The room was huge and empty. The only people present were the lawyers, a few journalists, two spectators who had received special permission to attend, and an imposing number of security personnel. Abdo and Mansuri were each in a barred cage, and were forced to stand during the two days the trial lasted; but, due to the way the cages were placed, they had to kneel in order to see the jurors. It was positively humiliating, and sent chills down my spine. My Italian colleagues appeared unmoved having, over the years, become inured to this system.

The trial took place on the 10th and 11th of October 1985. I was also supposed to defend Mansuri, who had only requested I represent him as the trial began. I had not been given permission to see him as he had been given an Italian attorney, and Joséphine could not contact him in prison to tell him to ask for my help. The boy I had met one year earlier in Trieste was now a sturdy, self-assured teenager. When he saw me, his face lit up. Although he talked to Joséphine during the rare recesses in the proceedings, throughout the length of the trial he would only say one word, *'Buongiorno'*.

On the other hand, Joséphine Abdo played an essential role in the trial. When the chief judge ordered her to take the witness-stand, and began questioning her in an attempt to elicit her name and learn something about her personality, she resolutely stood mute. But after the lawyers had made their closing statements and she turned to face the jury to defend herself, she impressed and, I believe, moved everyone. She expressed her political convictions, calling herself an 'Arab activist' without ever assuming responsibility for any of the violence that had occurred in Italy. That seemingly frail and defenceless girl vividly described the conditions in which she had been held, and insisted that little by little the total isolation, sensory deprivation, white cell walls, silence, lack of natural light, with a camera permanently aimed at her for sole company, had deprived her of her human dignity. Ever since the Baader-Meinhof trials in Germany the theme may sound familiar, but the Italian jurors reacted strongly, in particular one woman who began to cry even though the day before she had appeared totally indifferent to Abdo's fate. And a reporter, who I suspect has no sympathy for the revolution, asked me, during a recess, to kiss my client for him.

My closing speech was short. It was more of a statement that I had written and translated the evening before, in which I again brought up the matter of the forged document in the Trieste trial, and took the magistrates to task. Evoking the rights of man and fundamental democratic principles, I baldly adjured them not to base their decision on a forged legal document merely in order to find these people guilty, people they knew nothing about. That line of defence terrified my Italian colleagues. They asked for a short adjournment before my closing arguments to try to dissuade me, convinced that at my second sentence the president of the court would stop me and charge me with contempt of court. In which case, I would be spending that night in Rebibia. I asked Joséphine for her opinion, indicating the general tenor of my speech, and the fact that I was placing the ball back in the judges' court by telling them that if they accepted the forged document as evidence they themselves would look like an armed gang, with the Penal Code as their weapon. Joséphine smiled: 'I'm already serving fifteen years for nothing,' she said. 'There's no use the same thing happening to you. You're more useful to us outside than in.'

So I watered down some of my phrases, retaining the main thrust of my argument. The jury and court deliberated only for a short while, perhaps ten minutes. To the great surprise of the Italian lawyers, the verdict was for complete acquittal on insufficient evidence. I don't cry easily, but I wept with joy as I embraced Josephine through the cage bars. She remained calm, and the next day told me she was happy but that other comrades were still being held in custody, or had been given long and 'unjust' sentences, and that she could not really be happy until all of them were free.

L.G. This all seems paradoxical. As an agent of the DGSE, employed in that capacity, you approached these cases as if you were a left-wing activist lawyer, and obtained acquittals. Was that among the Service's objectives?

J.P.M. I am a defence counsel, and when I plead a case I think only of my clients, their liberty, and their future. That is my profession, and I invest myself in it totally. At such moments you feel that, by an inflection of your voice or with a particularly telling phrase you may be holding your client's past and future in your hands. That is the exciting part of it, the dramatic, gambling side of the legal profession. It would have been humanly impossible, worse, unthinkable, for me to have cheated. The Service had not given me any particular instructions, but even if 'they' had ordered me to 'find a way' to see to it that the sentences were heavier than normal, I would have ignored them. I was playing several roles: lawyer, secret agent, and so on, but I never failed to carry out my mission as defence lawyer, either in Italy, or in the Abdallah case. I wanted to contribute to deterring future terrorist attacks, but that would not stop me fighting for a defendant, and respecting the great principles of the law.

This time, everything went well. It must be said that the DGSE was holding all the cards. Even if acquitted, Abdo and Mansuri would still have to serve the fifteen- and sixteen-year prison sentences inflicted on them in Trieste. I had so few illusions about the workings of the Italian justice system, not to mention government policies, that I, with the other lawyers, appealed against the verdict handed down in Rome. Why? You must realize that in Italy, contrary to French judicial practice, the defendant may appeal against the verdict. And if he feels the verdict is wrong the prosecutor, too, may appeal 'in the public interest'. Knowing the acquittal would not suit the Italian government and that if we did not, the prosecution would, we entered the appeal that our clients had been acquitted for 'insufficient evidence', meaning they were given the benefit of the doubt, while we had asked for an acquittal, pure and simple. It may appear an audacious move, but it was a simple tactical manoeuvre. And Abdo and Mansuri had not yet been brought before the Trieste Assizes Court for the second time.

L.G. What was the FARL attitude towards you as a consequence of the outcome of the Rome trial?

J.P.M. Before the Rome trial, the mere fact that I was defending Abdo and Mansuri had brought me back into a state of grace. I had renewed contact with Abdallah in mid-May, and there was an unexpected telephone contact with 'Nathalie', a.k.a. Jacqueline Esber, on August 8th. She was worried about the danger to her friends during the Rome trial. On that occasion, and from time to time afterwards, I again served as messenger between her and Georges. As well-informed as ever, he had warned me in advance that 'Nathalie' would re-establish contact with me, and also said: 'I have good news concerning you.' He was alluding to his comrades' investigation of me.

Also, and Georges had warned me about this too, around that time I began receiving letters, six in all, bearing the name 'Lola Jiminez' on the back of the envelope, but with no return address. 'Those letters are meant for me,' Georges told me, 'don't open them. I'll make sure they weren't intercepted, myself.' The Service did not open the first one, even after passing it through an X-ray machine, but I think 'they' did open the others, even though Georges didn't seem to notice anything. He would read the letters in my presence, rip them into little pieces, literally the size of confetti, and hand them back to me saying, 'Throw this out.' A pretty puzzle for the Service's specialists.

With the Rome acquittal my reputation as a lawyer reached its peak within the group. I received three international money orders from Lebanon, drawn on the Indo-Suez Bank, and the Franco-Lebanese Bank, totalling fifty thousand francs, and signed by 'Nathalie Sber', a more than somewhat transparent alias. The Service told me this was characteristic of the Arab mentality. I had done my work well, so they were paying me accordingly. I could sense a change in the tone of my contacts with both Georges and 'Nathalie'. They were talking to me less as a lawyer who knew how to get out of a ticklish situation, than as an activitist who could be used as was necessary. Which suited the Service, since I found myself being used all over the place by the FARL.

L.G. Was that the end of your involvement with the Italian legal system?

J.P.M. Immediately after the Rome trial came the trial of the seven or eight militants arrested for the attempted bomb attack on the American embassy in Rome.* I did not take part in that, but in conformity with democratic judicial practice they were given very light sentences, for lack of sufficient evidence.

Another episode intrigued the Service, although I could never come to any definitive conclusions regarding it. This was the hijacking of the Italian cruiseship *Achille Lauro*, outside Port Said, Egypt, which occurred just prior to the Rome trial.† On the surface the attack, responsibility for which was claimed by Abou Abbas' PLF, a left-wing branch of Yassir Arafat's PLO, had nothing to do with the FARL. Not much was said about it in France, but I was preparing my case in Rome at the time and the Italian radio and television networks broadcast bulletin after bulletin explaining the pirates' demands. These were the release of all Arab 'political prisoners' in Italy, although the only names specifically mentioned were Abdo and Mansuri. I don't believe it had a bearing on the Rome verdict, since the hijacking was over before the hearing ended, and the jurors were no longer liable to blackmail. What was more interesting were the possible links between the PLF and the FARL, but it was impossible to find out exactly, at least I couldn't. Georges, whose release was not one of the PLF's demands, never said anything to me about the PLO, which is the official representative of the Palestinians. And I did not bring up the subject with Abdo.

L.G. How soon after the Rome trial did you return to Italy?

J.P.M. I went back to Italy about once a month, between October 1985 and March 1986, working on the appeal, which was being held in Trieste. I had to visit eight different prisons in order to see Joséphine Abdo! Slowly, her living conditions improved. She had subscribed to a Lebanese daily newspaper and seemed to be receiving more detailed news of the Middle-East situation than Georges was, for example. Partly, I think, she was being kept informed by the Red Brigades, thanks to revolutionary solidarity.

* See p.80.

† On 7 October 1985.

The second Trieste trial had initially been set for 30 January 1986, but was postponed due to the weather. There was so much snow that they were unable to transfer Abdo and Mansuri in time. The delay was sufficient for me to prepare their defence. The trial was rescheduled for March 10th, which meant I had constant contact with Italy, through Abdo, between July 1985 and March 1986. Just before the trial was to open in Trieste I was deluged in my hotel room with a series of telephone calls from Jacqueline Esber. She was extremely nervous, and had already telephoned me many times before the trial was rescheduled, unable to comprehend how the bad weather could justify a delay. She saw it as a political manoeuvre, which clearly annoyed her.

In March, when she called again, she seemed certain that Abdo and Mansuri would be released, acquitted as they had been in Rome and for the same reasons. I was not to return to Paris at the end of the trial, but was to accompany the two militants to Damascus, on a visa I had applied for, and been granted, after having explained precisely my reasons to the Syrian consulate in Paris!

The day before the trial opened Joséphine Abdo told me she had received a visit from an Italian magistrate, who had come to inquire to which country she intended to go once she was free! Alas, the trial did not turn out as well as had the one in Rome. My closing arguments were identical to those in the Rome trial, as were my colleagues', but the court's initial decision remained unaltered. In spite of deliberations that lasted two hours, and led to many telephone calls being made, Mansuri's sixteen-year sentence was confirmed, as was Abdo's fifteen-year term, and Ferial's *in absentia*. As at the first trial, the charges against Esber were dropped.

Things were starting to go badly for me again. Over the telephone, Esber became extremely abusive, accusing me of not having done my work properly. As if an activist lawyer could never lose a case! Once more the FARL, like the Service, was judging me on results obtained. I was very depressed when I returned to Paris, and had the impression that even though I had played all my cards, I had been banging my head against a wall. The Service did not seem surprised. When I left for Trieste, 'they' had told me that 'everything had been arranged'. Rather naively I assumed that this pointed to an acquittal, when obviously it meant just the opposite!

There was nothing left for me to do but to report to Abdallah. He did not reproach me, but became violently angry when I told him of Esber's heated diatribes against me. He thought she was 'crazy' to endanger my safety by openly calling me in my hotel room, and he dictated an appropriate message for me to transmit to 'Nathalie' as soon as she telephoned me in Paris, as planned.

'My wife is dirty,' the message read, 'she must take her clothes to the laundry.' He insisted heavily on '*the* laundry', rather than '*a* laundry'. But I did not deliver this message: Esber never called again.

|9|
THE REVOLUTIONARIES

By early 1986, and especially after the failure of the Trieste appeals, Jean-Paul Mazurier's relationship with the FARL was producing less and less of real value to the DGSE. However, he was still in contact with other left-wing activists. He had, reluctantly, agreed to act for Frédéric Oriach again, and in January 1986 he was asked to take on the defence of Pierre Carette, leader of the Belgian CCC (Cellules Combattantes Communistes), the group which had claimed responsibility for a number of attacks on NATO bases.

Jean-Paul Mazurier I was now involved only intermittently in the Abdallah case, whenever the imprisoned militants, Georges or Abdo, called on me for a specific mission. But the Service felt I might be useful in other ways as I was still Frédéric Oriach's defence counsel, and had also become Pierre Carette's lawyer. Carette was the leader of the Belgian CCC, the Communist Combatant Cells.

Laurent Gally When did you first meet Carette?

J.P.M. Oriach introduced me to him in, probably, 1982. I don't remember exactly, but it was while he was still at large. We made an appointment to meet him in a cafe. As far as I was concerned, Oriach was bringing me there to meet a 'comrade' whose ideas did not interest me. I don't even remember if he introduced Carette as being an activist publisher from Brussels, but his links with Action Directe were not mentioned. If I had been a 'revolutionary of

112

consequence', I would have known about it, but it was only after his arrest, when I read his police record, that I learned he had been head of DOCOM, the Communist Documentation Organization,* if memory serves. And I also learned that Carette had published tracts crediting and justifying the FARL for some of its actions in 1982, notably the machine-gun attack on the Israeli purchasing office in Paris.

It may seem hard to believe, but when I met Carette for the first time – I would not see him again until his arrest – I knew nothing about him and I had absolutely no interest in his activities. That day I was witness to one of Oriach's frenzies, but I was becoming used to them. After we finished our ritual coffee he insisted that he wanted the three of us to draw up 'a common platform, or thinking paper, for revolutionary action in Europe'. It took more self-control than usual for me to say nothing and not burst out laughing, but he seemed so excited by the idea that I allowed him to ramble on. Carette didn't seem any keener on the idea than I was. The only practical result of that meeting was that as we left the bistro, Carette borrowed one hundred francs from me!

L.G. Do you still have a low opinion of Carette?

J.P.M. No, on the contrary. A few weeks after his arrest, around the middle of January, 1986, he sent me a letter in which he designated me as his defence counsel. When I went to see him in Brussels' Saint-Gilles Prison I didn't remember having met him before. We had several long discussions, during which he explained the thrust of his struggle. Carette had no worldwide ambitions as did, for example, Oriach. His primary target was 'international capitalism', and the 'imperialist' American influence in Belgium, reflected primarily in the NATO presence there.

At the time, the media shared the general public psychosis. According to them, and it hasn't changed, the CCC was a common offshoot of Action Directe and Germany's Red Army Faction, and was committing, with impunity, a whole series of attacks capable of compromising the security of the 'Free World', since they were

* A revolutionary 'publishing house' used by Action Directe, with its printing press in Belgium.

directed against NATO. This babbling infuriated Carette, who explained that he had acted on his own, with only two other 'comrades' to help him carry out his first terrorist campaign: ten attacks perpetrated between October 1984 and May 1985. Carette was careful to explain the reasons behind his actions; on 1 May 1985 the CCC released a forty-eight-page communiqué!

L.G. Why did you tend to believe Carette?

J.P.M. It was a matter of common sense: go to the source. And my opinion was very quickly confirmed by the evidence in the dossier. There wasn't even a trace of Action Directe, or the Red Army Faction, for example. Carette had told me, in detail, that all the CCC attacks were carried out with explosives coming from one single source. That was an enormous quantity of explosives, more than eight hundred kilograms, I believe, and he told me how it had been 'liberated'. The group of militants trying to steal the explosives was so ill-equipped for this type of operation, and security at the mine where the explosives were stored left so much to be desired, that they made four trips over a three-week period to take them. You must not think the CCC was hated or feared in Belgium. Carette could flatter himself that the readers of a rock magazine had voted him the second most popular person of the year in Belgium, after Madonna!

L.G. How did you manage to get close to him?

J.P.M. By the usual tactics. The Service saw me as someone to deal with that sort of tangled revolutionary web, and left it up to me to unravel it. Carette had refused to appear at the questioning sessions, refused to answer the examining magistrate's summons, and also refused to appear before the Council Chamber, the Belgian judicial body that meets once a month to decide whether a prisoner is to be kept in custody or not. Since I was only one of his defence lawyers, legally I had nothing to do except maintain contact with my client.

The Belgian prosecutor kept things in perspective. The Carette case would remain a matter for the summary jurisdiction tribunal, and not the Assizes where criminal cases are tried. Still, Carette was facing one or even two ten-year sentences.

Pierre Carette knew me as Oriach's lawyer, and knew that I was defending Abdallah. He trusted me, and soon instructed me to telephone two of his comrades, members of the Red Line Collective, an absolutely legal support committee that served to explain the CCC's actions. I saw them three times, in Paris and in Brussels. One of them was ready to give up 'all that' and settle down. The other was a young woman about to give birth. They were obviously small-fry, there was no evidence against them, and it was as much through a sense of duty as because I knew there was nothing solid that could be held against them, that I gave their names to the Service. I used them as a communications channel, but even though they gave me names of other militants, those people never got in touch with me.

Later I learned that one person had been arrested and was accused of being a member of the CCC, but I never learned any more than their first names. I had turned over my information to the Service but I am certain I was not the cause of that arrest. The Belgian police had been after the CCC for a long time, and the investigators could not have had any problems infiltrating the Red Line, which operated openly. Several among them, including Carette, were caught by their own carelessness. They paid their rent, and some personal expenses, with cheques written on a bank account held jointly by several of the activists, which was rather conspicuous. My role was not to get people arrested; that would have been stupid for it would have broken many of the links that might lead us to information.

L.G. Since the CCC had targeted NATO bases, its members must also have been tracked by the Americans, especially the CIA.

J.P.M. That's self-evident. I never had any official confirmation of it but during conversations, or interviews, with American journalists in Paris, I noticed they were more interested in Carette than in Abdallah. To them, the FARL case seemed more a matter of principle as to the relations between European nations and Middle-Eastern movements, to do with the firmness which democratic countries must display. But the CCC represented an internal enemy who was, in a way, attacking them within their own fiefdom.

L.G. What does Carette look like?

J.P.M. He's a hale, vigorous type. Pierre, as the Belgians call him, radiates openness. He has complete faith in his own actions, and smiles constantly. He laughed heartily while telling me about stealing the explosives, recounting the story as if it were an ethnic joke, intensifying his Belgian accent until I felt as if I were listening to a stand-up comic!

Carette is also rather a megalomaniac; his telling me about the popularity poll which compared him to Madonna proves it. But he is truly popular. Learning that I was Carette's French lawyer, the taxi driver bringing me to the prison told me a story that is symptomatic. Carette, he said, comes to the Pearly Gates and is met by Saint Peter, who asks him his name.

'Peter,' Carette answers, certain that he is just as famous as the saint. Saint Peter looks in his book, frowns, and says: 'I'm sorry, you can't come in. Your name is not among the chosen.'

'You've made a mistake, old man,' says Carette. 'I've just come to warn you that you have fifteen minutes to clear out the place. It's going to blow up.'

I laughed at the joke, but it illustrated the care the CCC took that no one should be hurt during their attacks. Excellent demolition experts, they had managed to blow up a bank without hurting anyone. They would send warnings ahead of time, either by distributing leaflets or by telephone, giving the employees time to flee. And if, in the end, there were two victims, it was because two 'unlucky firemen', as Carette called them, were sent to the target site by the police, despite warnings to evacuate everybody.

L.G. You're visibly sympathetic towards Carette, and the CCC's methods. Didn't your attitude bother the Service?

J.P.M. My feelings and the Service's needs didn't always coincide: far from it. I was nervous that the role I was playing – and which I had intended to be the prevention of FARL attacks in France, and only that – had slowly evolved into a wide-ranging, repressive one. Although I did not share Carette's ideas, I did not find what he was doing distasteful. And it did happen, at times, that I would 'forget' to transmit certain information if it did not coincide with my own objectives.

Carette was very clear about what he was doing. He thoroughly disapproved of the attacks carried out, or for which responsibility was claimed, by the CSPPA, the Committee for Solidarity with Arab and Near-Eastern Political Prisoners, at the end of 1985 and beginning of 1986.* He felt that innocent people should never be the target of an attack, no matter for what reasons. He even blamed me for having attempted to justify those attacks in the press, as well as to him, in my official role as Abdallah's lawyer/friend/accomplice, even though it was with the Service's approval.

'How can you defend people like that?' Carette asked, almost accusingly. Following that same reasoning, he had considered naming *Maître* Jacques Vergès as one of his defence lawyers but quickly changed his mind, not wanting to call on 'Klaus Barbie's lawyer'.

L.G. What were the links between Carette and Abdallah?

J.P.M. None existed. Carette had never met Georges, I'm sure of that. On the other hand, he knew members of Action Directe, the German Red Army Faction, and the Italian Red Brigades. It seems like a lot of people; but Carette never ceased claiming he was a 'Belgian revolutionary', and didn't need anyone else. He was very jealous of his independence. As uncontested head of the CCC, he even went so far as to tell me, 'The CCC, that's me.' Pierre thought the press reports claiming that Oriach had inspired the CCC's methods were both unjust and unfounded. When I left he said, rather coldly, that I should convey a message of solidarity to Abdallah.

L.G. What did Abdallah think of Carette?

J.P.M. He could 'appreciate' the CCC's actions, while at the same time judging them to be 'a bit soft'. As early as 1982, Georges had dreamed of a great internationalist revolutionary movement. Even though the CCC was aiming its actions primarily at NATO bases, with their strong American connections, Georges felt Carette's motives were too exclusively nationalistic. Also, Carette had come out openly against armed struggle. Georges never gave me

* This series of bomb attacks in Paris is described in chapter 10. See also Appendix, pp.196-7.

any messages for Brussels. But this opinion was not shared by Joséphine Abdo, who spoke admiringly of the CCC actions. She asked me to give Carette assurances of her friendship and fraternal feelings, as well as from the members of the Red Brigades who were incarcerated in the same prison with her. But, according to both Abdallah and Abdo herself, she was not involved in any FARL actions in Europe.

L.G. Were there strong ties between Carette and Oriach?

J.P.M. They had known each other a long time and kept up a steady correspondence during Oriach's imprisonment, from autumn 1982 until spring 1986. The letters I mailed for Oriach, to Belgium, were first read by the Service. Carette thought Oriach a chronic hysteric and once, in talking about the explosives still held by the CCC, laughingly said: 'When Frédéric is released the comrades will send him some, but only one gram at a time because he might rush into the first synagogue he sees, and set off some fireworks!' I could sense a basic disagreement between the two militants, but that did not keep the effusive Carette from having friendly feelings towards Oriach.

L.G. What was your relationship with Oriach while he was in prison?

J.P.M. Going to see him was a chore. Oriach could talk of nothing except politics, and in the most abstract manner conceivable. I was bored, could not concentrate, and looked for any reason I could to leave. Between 1982 and 1984 I felt so little sympathy for him that I refused to defend him, and only saw him again on Abdallah's orders – and for the needs of the Service. About once a week I would drag myself to the prison. After Oriach had been on hunger strike, I even had to act as his grocery delivery-boy. That was last year, when he had fasted for a month and a half, probably. When it ended he was exhausted, and I brought him meat and cheese on the sly so he could regain his strength. My mother cooked the snacks, which were meant to supplement the food the prison administration was giving him. To put a hunger striker back on his feet, they usually feed him starchy food. It was only after his release – which was absolutely legal, but which irritated a great many people in the new government – that I realized how physically screwed up Oriach was. I wondered whether he mightn't have had polio when he was a child, considering his large legs, small torso, and hydrocephalic head. I'm not being very nice about him, but he had a talent for infuriating me, constantly repeating the same revolutionary and one-worldist speeches.

L.G. Did Oriach like Carette?

J.P.M. Yes. He was 'a brother', as the expression goes, but a brother of whom he warned me to be careful. To Oriach's mind, a lawyer is a professional whose job it is to pull his clients out of their legal messes the best way he can. In no case must a defence lawyer become a militant. 'Be careful,' he would say, 'Carette will surely ask you to do something for his movement. Don't do a thing.' That seems like basic good sense, but Oriach was suspicious of what he called 'the Baader School', that is, the West German terrorists who had a tendency to ask their lawyers to go far beyond their normal roles. Exactly as Abdallah had asked me to, in 1982, when he wanted to use my office as a meeting place for his comrades.

L.G. Did Oriach admire Abdallah?

J.P.M. To him, Georges was almost a living god. Oriach was very flattered when the FARL, planning their 'world-wide' operation of 15 October 1984, announced that his release constituted one of their primary objectives. Before that Frédéric had been more or less a lone wolf and appeared very isolated, even during the first incarnation of Action Directe, around 1981-2. He felt great solidarity with that movement, but no more than that.

Afterwards, I told Oriach of Georges' wish that he take part in that famous internationalist revolutionary movement which was Abdallah's prime objective. Oriach looked as if he had just been promoted Marshal of the Army: the only French activist deemed worthy of standing beside the Middle-Eastern brotherhood, sacred bearers of the Palestinian cause! And the fact that Georges also counted me among his future troops made me worthy of his trust. In a sense, I could understand his feelings. Until that point, he had merely written about the Palestinian cause. Now his own writing, his own reasoning, had attracted their attention, and he would be allowed to go into action. In prison, he once showed me a very long article about him that had appeared in the left-wing Lebanese newspaper, *As Safir*. The headline read: 'Frédéric Oriach is in prison for us.'

L.G. Did Oriach ask anything of Abdallah?

J.P.M. In order to receive the benefit of his advice, and his approval, Oriach would send Abdallah his theoretical writings through me. Some of Oriach's writings on Palestine were even found in the Rue Lacroix safe house where the DST discovered the FARL weapons cache. After Abdallah's arrest the two men wrote to each other directly. But in order to get past the prison censor Oriach would give his most 'sensitive' letters to me. The Service would read them first, then Georges would read them, a sarcastic smile on his lips. But he never answered, only commenting, 'It's not bad. He's about the only one who has grasped the nature of the Palestinian problem, even though he has not yet assimilated the Arab mentality.'

Just before his release Oriach began worrying about his future, and decided to return to being an activist as quickly as possible. He was invited officially, by certain public organizations, to go to Syria and he approached Georges about the problem of how to get there. Could he travel semi-officially but still meet some of the comrades? Georges sent him a message of the same order as those he had given me for 'Nathalie'.

'The first girlfriend must approach a third party to have a second girlfriend quickly. And it will be almost directly. Greetings.'

The 'almost' was underlined three times. Translation: Oriach was to wait to be contacted directly by the comrades. Sensing Oriach's impatience after his release, Georges instructed me to go and see him and dot all the i's and cross all the t's. Instead of taking the first plane leaving for Damascus, Oriach was to go to any Eastern-European country and wait to be contacted directly.

L.G. Which emphasizes the freedom of movement, if not the direct support, the FARL receives from the Iron Curtain countries.

J.P.M. Yes. But even though Oriach was free, he was under twenty-four-hour surveillance by the police, who dreaded his impulsiveness. After telling me the story about the synagogue into which Oriach supposedly would dash, Carette also told me that if

Frédéric ever saw a little old lady being struck by a hit-and-run driver, he would strangle the driver.

L.G. In practical terms, what profit did the *Piscine* derive from this Carette-Oriach-Abdallah triangle?

J.P.M. I'm not the *Piscine*; I'm only a 'lifeguard'! In my opinion, everything I was reporting seemed essential. The Service's stock-in-trade, their very reason for being, is the totality of intelligence (not all of which need be spectacular) that helps define whether or not there is any activity, and if something must be done to contain any operations that might be in preparation.

By the beginning of December 1986, except for one meeting at my office after his return from Syria, I had not seen Oriach for about three months. This does not mean that our lines of communication have been cut: Georges' behaviour has accustomed me to the militants' changeability.

As for Carette, I have just received a letter from him in which he thanks me for my past efforts and informs me that I am no longer his lawyer. I went to see him for what I now believe may have been the last time, in mid-November, and virtually gave him an ultimatum. Our recent meetings had been unproductive, he had not provided me with any new information, and I warned him that due to the increasingly repressive atmosphere I was considering going underground. Therefore, I needed contacts as even though the comrades knew me I myself had no idea whom to approach. Carette promised to think it over. He finally chose not to tell me anything more.

|10|
THE AUTUMN OF LIVING DANGEROUSLY

During the winter of 1985/86 a series of bomb attacks took place in Paris. They were claimed by a mysterious group calling itself the CSPPA, the Comité de Solidarité avec les Prisonniers Politiques Arabes et du Proche Orient *(Committee for Solidarity with Arab and Near-Eastern Political Prisoners). One of the CSPPA's demands was the freeing of Abdallah. What, if any, was the group's connection with the FARL? A series of letters received by Mazurier for Abdallah appeared to contain some clues.*

Jean-Paul Mazurier After mid-October 1985, and the acquittal at the Rome Assizes, I had begun receiving messages through the post.

Some of the letters, sent from Lebanon or Syria, came directly to my office. On the back, the sender's name read 'Lola Jiminez'. Abdallah had told me in advance about these letters and ordered me not to open them. Of course the Service did not heed his request. The postmarks puzzled the *Piscine*: theoretically, those four or five envelopes were all posted in Paris the day before I received them. The obvious answer was that for some reason the postmarks had been forged and that a comrade had hand-delivered them directly to my concierge's mailbox. But we were never able to prove it, and 'they' were not telling me anything. Were those letters from Jacqueline Esber to Abdallah?

Again, towards the end of October 1985, I received two letters mailed in the Paris region and addressed to me at my office. Inside was some money: one thousand francs, in one envelope; two or three hundred thousand lira in the other. And each time an almost identical message: 'Please remit this modest sum to our imprisoned comrades, as a sign of solidarity.' I gave the francs to Abdallah but he handed them back to me, saying: 'You need this more than I do.' I turned over the lira to Abdo when I went to visit her in Italy. The letters were unsigned, and on the back of each envelope were words with which the French have become very familiar: 'Committee for Solidarity with Arab and Near-Eastern Political Prisoners', the CSPPA.

Laurent Gally Which was, according to you, the same nebulous committee that later claimed credit for the bombing attacks in Paris during the winter of 1985 and 1986?

J.P.M. At the time, we knew nothing about them. The explosions began in December 1985, with bombings at the Galeries Lafayette and Printemps department stores. The *brigade criminelle* which investigates crimes of violence, at first thought they were the work of a madman. When the CSPPA went public they first used the name 'The Committee for Solidarity with Arab and Near-Eastern Political Prisoners'. The addition of the words 'Near-Eastern' undoubtedly came from the fact that the CSPPA was demanding not only Abdallah's release, but also that of Warujian Garabedjian, an Armenian belonging to the ASALA, and of Anis Naccache, a Lebanese Shiite Muslim.

At the time I received those two letters I remember thinking that the messages, which were awkwardly handwritten on a leaf torn from a shorthand notebook, seemed rather 'thin'. I didn't know who those people were but they didn't seem to be a particularly well-organized group. The name did not surprise me. Several months earlier Abdallah had said that since French 'revolutionaries' were so inactive he had created, inside his own prison and others, an internal network prisoners could use to communicate with each other and broadcast their demands, or political positions, to the outside world.

He also told me that in the summer of 1985 Radio Mouvance, a pirate radio station focussed on prison-system issues and prisoners' problems, had refused to broadcast a text he sent them regarding the Palestinian issue. This text, writted by Georges himself, and for which he had obtained endorsements from other prisoners (he did not give me their names) was signed, if one could believe him, with an acronym very similar to the CSPPA.

I didn't attach much importance to what he was saying at that moment; so little, that I didn't even inform the Service. Apparently Abdallah was furious that Radio Mouvance, whose broadcasts to the convict population were extremely popular inside prison – another fact I had to explain to the Service – was approaching the Palestinian issue in a way he deemed unacceptable. I will not go into the details. On the whole, Abdallah was protesting against Radio Mouvance's political stance, which he considered to be under Frédéric Oriach's influence. Oriach had stated publicly that a Jew was not necessarily a Zionist. Abdallah always believed otherwise, and considered that statement 'anti-revolutionary'.

The relationship between Abdallah and Oriach, or his friends, was bizarre. In 1984, with Oriach already in jail and Abdallah about to re-establish contact with me before his arrest in Lyons, something very revealing occurred. One evening, Frédéric Oriach's support committee held a meeting in Paris. As you would expect, the meeting hall was overrun with members of police intelligence. And then, as several people later told me, a man stepped forward and shouted to the speakers: 'Good evening, I am here to declare the FARL's revolutionary support for Frédéric Oriach, who has been imprisoned unjustly. We would like to make contact with him.' As you can see, the method was not particularly discreet. 'Alex' had already asked me to establish contact for him with Oriach, and here was another of the group's members publicly asking the same thing. Georges later told me it was a personal initiative on the man's part, and that it cast a chill over the meeting.

Later, a comrade who set up a meeting with that FARL member, 'in order to explore the subject further', didn't show up. Affronted that the FARL militant had been 'stood up', Georges questioned me as to that comrade's reliability. I didn't know her and was forced to calm him down when he began talking about 'eliminating her' for being a threat to the group's security. I don't know what conclusions the police intelligence people might have reached after this incident or what leads they were able to develop.

L.G. Let's get back to the CSPPA for a moment. What were the Service's thoughts on this group, after the first bombings in December?

J.P.M. I don't believe the *Piscine* ever succeeded in identifying any member of the group from the cover name on the envelopes I received. Along with those two letters was a package containing three books in Arabic, apparently Marxist political essays, that I later gave to Abdallah to help fill the long hours. The important point is that not long ago, I think it was in September 1986, or some time later, the Service told me that the handwriting on one of the statements claiming responsibility for the bombings that occurred that month had been identified as being identical to the handwriting on the two letters signed by the CSPPA sent in October 1985. But those are the only details I have on the subject.

L.G. But this is of prime importance. You are claiming that the CSPPA was in existence as early as October 1985, and may be the same group that a year later claimed responsibility for at least one bombing in Paris, in September 1986. That contradicts your suggestion that the CSPPA, with the small means at its disposal, is an external branch of Abdallah's efforts to co-ordinate the political struggle from inside prison.

J.P.M. I don't know if that is the same group, but I do remember that the CSPPA began claiming credit for bombing attacks carried out in Paris in February 1986: the Claridge Gallery bombing on the Champs-Elysées, the Gibert Jeune bookstore bombing on Boulevard Saint-Michel, and the bombing at Fnac-Forum, the discount store in the Halles, and so on, as well as later claiming responsibility for the bombings at the Galeries Lafayette and Printemps department stores. After that first series of bombings at the beginning of 1986, Georges told me that the attacks might have been carried out by a group with only limited resources, and that the techniques they used, which were relatively simple, would allow them to continue waging their campaign for six months, at the rate of one bomb explosion a day, if they wanted.

L.G. Was this one of Abdallah's daydreams, or was he basing his theories on descriptions of the explosions that had appeared in the press? Or did he have private sources of information, which he revealed to you?

J.P.M. I had the impression that Georges learned quite a lot on his own. After the Rome trial, probably in November 1985, there was a message from Jacqueline Esber to Abdallah, one sentence, which was unusual, saying: 'The books will arrive.' I drew no conclusions from it: this message was sent after I received the three books from the CSPPA for Georges, but it was long before the 1986 bombing of the Gibert bookstore.

On the other hand, Abdallah did ask me to talk to the press at the beginning of February 1986, to declare that those first bombings were probably only a warning and that it would be illogical not to expect widespread Arab solidarity regarding the Abdallah case. The Service authorized me to broadcast his opinions, and I was interviewed on the France-Inter radio network, where I said that in my considered opinion, other, more murderous attacks might soon be shedding French blood. The next day the newspaper *France-Soir* made that their headline, and Pierre Joxe, then Interior Minister, went on the radio to reply that the government would not allow its conduct to be dictated by a lawyer. The episode led to quite a lot of trouble for me. The bar council expressed its unease and, more than ever, I was regarded by them as a terrorist lawyer.

L.G. In your statements, were you repeating Abdallah's message exactly? Had it been dictated to you, word for word, by the Service, or did you yourself go overboard? Why did you talk about other, more murderous bombings?

J.P.M. I was repeating Abdallah's remarks. The Service had given me the go ahead to talk to the press but had not dictated what I was to say. I was to be concise, detached, even if what I was saying was brutal. I quickly realized that, carried away by enthusiasm, I had gone too far. Jean-Pierre Elkabbach, on radio station Europe 1, even called me 'an accomplice', live, on the air. The day after the interview, having realized its repercussions, the Service formally forbade me any contact with the press.

Georges was ecstatic, and informed me that my entire interview had been broadcast in Lebanon. Only one thing was bothering him, a sentence he had, of course, dictated to me and that France-Inter had edited out. On his orders I had declared that 'Israel is a European colony installed in Arab territory.'

Thinking back, I still wonder if when Abdallah was talking about Arab solidarity regarding his case he was referring to a majority of the Arab immigrants living in France, or only to the CSPPA militants. Or was he referring, more generally, to the countries of the Near East, and the Arab people as a whole, or to their progressive or extremist factions? Any one of those possibilities is conceivable, but Abdallah often complained of the inertia displayed by his brother Arabs living in France, and would always repeat the same theme: 'There are almost three million of them living here permanently, and I haven't received a single letter of support from any of them.'

L.G. You were discussing the CSPPA at the beginning of October 1985. They were not complete unknowns since, in his last book, Jacques Toubon, secretary-general of the RPR (*Rassemblement pour la République*, the Gaullist party), mentions they had already been spotted by that time. But didn't the wave of bombings in Paris in February and March, 1986, mark the failure of your, and the Service's, supposedly deterrent activities?

J.P.M. Certainly, and the failure was a grave one but, perhaps, explicable. In March 1985, with the plans for exchanging Georges for Gilles Sidney Peyroles, the Abdallah case became an affair of state. The general public was not told, but the government knew how potentially dangerous the case might become, as it had already demanded the involvement and mediation of several foreign countries, notably Algeria. Although I believe I had regained Abdallah's trust before the wave of bombings began in the winter of 1985 (proof of which are the many messages I carried for him) it is probable that the internal channels of communication within the FARL, or among its accomplices, had been altered. Georges had been in jail for more than a year and probably had begun losing control of his group. In my opinion, if he was still kept informed of any attacks being planned it was not necessarily through me. Knowing that my 'carelessness' had probably led to the Italian raids at the beginning of December 1984, the group had reduced my role: trusting me didn't necessarily imply telling me everything.

Before that first wave of bombings occurred I believe I provided the Service with another path of inquiry, perhaps the most important of all. In November and December 1985, I received a third series of letters. An envelope arrived at my office bearing a postmark from Corbeil-Essones, outside Paris. Inside the envelope were two letters carrying Syrian postage stamps, and an illegible postmark. The letters were addressed to a certain Ouadilene Saoudi, 4 Rue de la Nacelle, Corbeil. The address, which was typed, had been completely obliterated with blue ink, but by holding the envelope up to the light I could read it. I was surprised at the ease with which I could read the name of the person who had received the letters from Syria and sent them on to me.

There was nothing special written on the French envelope, not even the name of the person who was meant ultimately to receive it. But one of the two Syrian letters, written in Arabic, was not sealed. The Service's translators went to work on it, and I later delivered both letters to Georges, who smiled as he read them. Was the Service able to trace the letters back, starting with that Saoudi person? Was the Corbeil address real; was it a hideout, a way station, or a 'mail drop'? Did those letters have any connection to those sent by the CSPPA? I was not kept abreast of developments based on the information I had obtained.

The Service cannot have destroyed the network: the Paris bombings of December, February and March prove that. But my role in this matter was no smaller, nor any less important than it had been one year earlier, during my first meetings with Esber. The *Piscine* was receiving most of the same information as Abdallah was; and if the bombing attacks were not foiled, it is because when those operations were being prepared they were not, or not properly, communicated to Georges in prison.

L.G. There were four bombings in one week. What was the Service's reaction to them?

J.P.M. The *Piscine* was under great pressure, but had no idea where to take action. One hour after the Claridge Gallery bombing on the Champs-Elysées, 'Antoine' telephoned me to announce the explosion and said: 'We have received a message from the PLF [Palestine Liberation Front], but can't tell if it's legitimate.' I didn't know what to think. My experiences in Italy, before the opening of the Rome trial, had brought this group to my attention. They were apparently an extremist arm of the PLO, and had claimed credit for hijacking the cruiseship, *Achille Lauro*. What 'Antoine' was suggesting was indeed possible: that some Palestinians might have committed the bombings so as to bring about Georges' release, as they may have done the preceding October, demanding the release of Abdo and Mansuri, along with the other 'Arab political prisoners' held in Italy.

I did what I could, and visited Abdallah in order to fish for information. As his lawyer, Georges assured me that he unreservedly supported any Arab action. As his militant comrade, he explained to me that he disapproved of the methods being used, bombs exploding in public and hitting innocent citizens, even if no one had died. This was his old theory of 'dirty' targets in which attacks claimed victims among the general public, and 'clean' targets, particular individuals chosen for their position, or their political opinions. The first incarnation of the FARL, at the beginning of 1982 in Paris, aimed at 'clean' targets. Georges did not suggest who the authors of those February bombings might be, but he appeared convinced the attacks would not help obtain his release.

It was at that moment I realized I would no longer get much out of Georges, as he was no longer giving me written messages except a few letters to Abdo, and contact with 'Nathalie' had again broken off. Knowing the visitors' room was infested with microphones, he could no longer speak openly. Any statements he now made were 'for the record'.

L.G. Had you begun to have doubts about the validity of your role?

J.P.M. Not yet. I was greatly disappointed at not having been able to foil any bombings, but I still had the impression I was waiting him out, gathering information, ant-like, through various channels and passing it on to the Service for action. Georges had taught me patience. 'Ten men armed with patience can conquer ten thousand men without,' he would say, citing an Arab proverb.

L.G. Didn't the bombings in early 1986 seem to you to be linked to the approaching Lyons trial,* an attempt to pressure the judges? Georges knew he would soon be coming to trial, and his freedom was at stake.

J.P.M. It's possible. The bombings put pressure on the government in general. The first bombing death, at the Point-Show Gallery on the Champs-Elysées,† occurred the same day Jacques Chirac was named to head the government. It could have meant three things: that the new team in power would have to make a quick decision about the Abdallah case; that the bombing might also have been a response to the confirmation of the guilty verdicts, ten days earlier, on Abdo and Mansuri, in Trieste; or that according to terrorist claims, France remained, among all the nations in Europe, the sole country considered to have any reponsibility in the FARL affair.

February passed, then March, and still no date was set for the trial in Lyons. The magistrate's investigation was long ended but it was the French government who would decide when the case would be brought to trial. The prosecutor still had to submit the written charges, and so on. One thing is certain: the Left did not want the trial to take place before the general election of March 1986, even though, technically, it could have done. So it turned out that the new government majority, whom everybody including the Left expected would win the election, would inherit the affair.

Georges seemed in no hurry to go to trial. He knew that his case, with all the moral connotations attached to terrorism, was dependent on the French legal system and also, if not primarily, on the decision of the government. He was becoming pessimistic for, at the beginning of 1986, in answer to Oriach's questions about his expectations for the immediate future, he said: 'Calm Frédéric down; he'll be out long before I will . . .' Therefore, the bombings did not tip the balance of power in his favour, far from it.

---

* Abdallah's first trial was to take place in Lyons in July 1986.
† 20 March 1986.

THE AUTUMN OF LIVING DANGEROUSLY

L.G. At the various times it claimed responsibility for bombings, the CSPPA was not only demanding Abdallah's release but also the release of pro-Khomeini Lebanese Anis Naccache, and Warujian Garabejian, head of the Armenian ASALA commando group that had carried out the armed attack at Orly Airport.*

J.P.M. I was not involved with those last two, and knew nothing about them beyond what was published in the press. In jail, Abdallah put together a collective report on the Palestinian Revolution, and told me he had received the consent of certain other prisoners. Which ones? Georges was astounded by those bombings and said: 'I don't understand why they're demanding the release of three people who have no connection with each other.' I think Garabejian and Naccache were mentioned as they were the most likely to be released, but the essential demand was Abdallah's freedom.

According to the Service, and other authorities, there are sometimes subtle differences between what terrorists demand and what is reported in the press. For example, during the Gilles Peyroles kidnapping in Lebanon, in March 1985, it was reported that the FARL had taken him so as to trade him for Abdallah. The DST, whose former head, Prefect Bonnet, wrote a long report on that affair, always claimed – and the Service confirmed it to me in part – that the FARL wanted not only Abdallah but also Mansuri and Oriach in exchange for Peyroles. That's an age-old tactic: ask for a lot in order to obtain at least the essential, which in this case was Georges. A tactic which the CSPPA might have been using in adding Garabejian and Naccache's names to that of Abdallah.

* A bomb exploded near the office of the Turkish airline in Orly Airport on 15 July 1983, leaving eight dead and fifty-four wounded. In 1985 Warujian Garabejian was sentenced to life imprisonment for his part in the attack.

|11| **BLACK SEPTEMBER**

Abdallah finally came up for trial in Lyons on 3 July 1986. He was sentenced to four years' imprisonment for criminal associations, using a forged passport, and possession of weapons. Abdallah, who had hoped to be freed, warned that there would be reprisals. Then, in September, a new and even bloodier series of bomb attacks began in Paris.

Jean-Paul Mazurier Between the bombing attacks of February and March 1986, and the infinitely bloodier, more sickening ones of September, Abdallah came to trial in the criminal court at Lyons. At last! I thought. The affair had already dragged on for more than twenty months. At nine in the morning, 3 July 1986, I entered the Assize Court, the only courtroom large enough to accommodate the crowd of reporters. The gendarmes had turned the courthouse into an armed camp. Remembering the trial of Bruno Bréguet and Magdalena Kopp, alleged henchmen of the terrorist Carlos, the authorities obviously feared an attack that day, although not necessarily here. Bréguet and Kopp had come to trial in Paris in 1981, only a few hours before the bomb attack on Rue Marbeuf. But the court had not allowed itself to be influenced; quite the contrary.

Laurent Gally Were you in contact with the prosecutors before the trial opened? Did you have any idea how severe the public prosecutor's charge would be, or how harsh the sentence he would demand?

132

J.P.M. Two days before the trial began I telephoned the deputy public prosecutor, the person who would be presenting the charges at the hearing. The general public is not usually aware that in an important trial the prosecution's charges are not always drawn up by the person who presents them at the hearing. It is often the public prosecutor himself, that is to say, the official head of all the prosecuting lawyers and, therefore, the chief accuser, who is author of the document. As for the sentence demanded after the reading of the charges, it is often determined – and this is perfectly legal – by the Justice Minister, or the most important members of the chancellery. It is they who, ultimately, represent the state and society, in whose name they may demand judgement against whoever they deem guilty, after having studied the case file established by the examining magistrate.

Abdallah was familiar with this sort of juridical reasoning, and found in it a further source for political rhetoric, telling me he would never be judged fairly, but only according to the *desiderata* of the French government. He still gave no weight to the independence of the judiciary. According to the French penal code, he was liable for up to ten years in prison on the main charge, 'associating with criminals'. He was also being accused of possession of weapons and explosives, and of the use of forged identity papers. Under French law, the only sentence that could be imposed was the maximum sentence on the main charge, contrary to the United States where sentences are cumulative, meaning that some criminals can be imprisoned for 135 years, for example, and not simply for life, as in France.

As a lawyer who had dealt with numerous similar cases, I concluded that, in practical terms, if Abdallah had been a normal 'client' he might be facing the average sentence, six years in prison. But this case, with its terrorist and political implications, was different. The deputy prosecutor seemed friendly enough over the telephone, our conversation lasted almost an hour, but he did not reveal what sort of sentence he would be requesting. I did most of the talking, warning the magistrate, explaining about the forged document on which the Italian trials were based, and the risk of reprisals that might follow too heavy a sentence, citing particularly the Point-Show bombing and his individual responsibility now that our country had become the main target of terrorists whom we had been unable to neutralize.

L.G. Were you speaking personally, as a lawyer, or had the Service suggested this tactic?

J.P.M. This was strictly personal. On the contrary, the Service was hoping Abdallah would be sent to prison for life. Nothing was standing in the way of it happening. If part of the case, apparently the most important part, was about to be judged in Lyons, still another part was taking place in Paris, in the office of Gilles Boulouque, the examining magistrate. And in Paris Abdallah's only attorney was *Maître* Vergès. There was also a third investigation of Georges lost in the sleepy judicial backwater of Strasbourg.* The fact that the case had been divided into three distinct parts, and five examining magistrates were attempting to sort it out, actually allowed the judicial system or, rather, the chancellery, a certain leeway in its actions in the face of changing circumstances. Let me explain. Abdallah could have been tried and sentenced three separate times, or only tried in Lyons with the other charges being dropped, and so on. In brief, the political powers-that-be had plenty of room to manoeuvre.

For my part, I thought that if they simply freed Abdallah at the end of the Lyons trial it would not exactly be glorious, but that such a move was justified in order to close a case which was becoming progressively trickier, and keep France from being caught up in the mechanism of terrorist reprisals. I did not discuss my approach to the deputy prosecutor in advance with *Maître* Vergès, any more than we had prepared a common defence.

It was the first time in my career I had ever telephoned the prosecuting counsel before a trial. I was conscious of the enormity of what I was doing, especially since I almost threatened him, making him more or less personally responsible, in advance, for

* The Paris inquiry arose from the discovery of the FARL weapons cache at 18 Rue Lacroix, see p.195. The Strasbourg investigation related to the attack on Robert Onan Homme, United States Consul General in Strasbourg, on 26 March 1984, see Appendix p.194.

any bombing attacks which might follow a guilty verdict. It was a gross impropriety, but considering my reputation in this affair I didn't have much to lose.

L.G. Had Abdallah led you to believe there would be reprisals if he were found guilty? Or did he hope to walk out of the courtroom a free man?

J.P.M. No, on the contrary. When Abdallah entered the court-room, his opening statement established the political basis of the trial, as if he were addressing not only the judges but public opinion, and the government, via the media. Impeccably dressed – he had even asked my advice on the matter, as if he was determined to make a good impression – Abdallah was calm, but aggressive. He refused to state his name when the president of the tribunal asked him to do so, and reaffirmed that he was an 'Arab combattant', before launching himself into an account of the tragedy of Lebanon, the effects of the civil war there and of French diplomacy in the region. His statement was far from original, but very clear: 'France must choose which camp it wants to be in,' he said, hammering out his words and, in fact, calling upon the court to carry out a government policy decision! In his mind, whatever the court's verdict might be it would have world-wide value as a diplomatic symbol.

Georges had a fairly clear idea of what his comrades' reactions would be. 'If I'm sentenced to two years,' he said the day before the trial, ' "they'll" keep quiet; but if they give me ten years, "they'll" go into action.' Obviously he did not believe he would be acquitted, but a two-year sentence would have immediately made him eligible for release, taking into account the time, twenty months, he had already served in custody. Yet at the same time, he knew he might be given the maximum, a ten-year sentence. He wanted the court to hand down either a minimum or a maximum sentence so that the government's attitude would be clear, and serve as a comprehensible signal to his comrades.

L.G. What was your role during the trial?

J.P.M. As Abdallah wanted, I was pugnacious and awkward. I repeated the story of the forged transcripts which had led to the Italian guilty verdicts, in an attempt to demonstrate that the evidence might thus have been tainted. This provoked an incident in the courtroom, when the deputy prosecutor objected to my 'inadmissible' manner of implicating the French legal establishment. He knew that was not the case, but the DST is rarely mentioned in court and everyone plays the game, the defence as well as the prosecution.

If I mention this incident it is because it was the only one that occurred during the trial. One might have thought he was among friends, all of whom were intent on smoothing things over to avoid any public display of disagreement. It was all fairly surrealistic. The president of the court was only too friendly to Abdallah, putting on a display of social graces, recognizing not only the defendant's right to enumerate his political beliefs, but also his right to refuse to explain the facts. The assistant deputy prosecutor read the charges in a dull voice. No one listened, since there was to be no argument. Everyone was waiting to hear the summing up, and what sentence would be demanded. It turned out to be a four-year prison term, *a priori* rather reasonable, when you consider the case from the prosecution's point of view.

Maître Vergès made a brilliant closing speech, calmly repeating Abdallah's arguments. Be careful, he seemed to be saying to the authorities, your decision will weigh heavily on the events that follow. The trial was wrapped up in under three hours. Some reporters were surprised it was cut so short, and at the lightness of the sentence, which appeared to have been handed down in advance to allow the case to be closed.

L.G. That impression is reinforced by an *a posteriori* reading of the Lyons charges. Abdallah was answering not only charges of criminal association and using a forged passport, but also of weapons possession in the matter of the Rue Lacroix arms cache. Which largely rid the Paris dossiers of all meaning.

J.P.M. There was no need, juridically, to include the Rue Lacroix weapons charge in the Lyons trial: far from it. But it helped support the charge of criminal association, as one can hardly imagine dangerous criminals not having weapons and explosives, and in this case those were the only weapons and explosives available to the prosecution. But including them in the

Lyons trial entailed a risk. How could they later charge Abdallah with complicity in murder in the second judicial investigation then in progress, in Paris, if the charge of 'possessing weapons used in the commission of a crime' was not upheld by the Lyons tribunal? The verdict, which the court was to deliver in a week, was of prime importance not only for the length of the sentence, but also for the enactment of that sentence which would either close, or carry over to, the Paris case.

The judges gave themselves a week to weigh up their decision. For what reason? I almost choked when I heard the president of the court justify the delay by saying: 'It will give my assistants, the assessors, time to familiarize themselves with the dossier.' What? An affair of this importance, and two out of three of the judges were taking part in the trial knowing nothing about it, except in the broadest terms? It was an aberration, but I believe the president of the court provided this excuse quickly so as not to be forced to admit that the court's decision would be a political one, and that he was asking for calm, if not for advice.

L.G. But the week between the end of the trial and the announcement of the verdict was not exactly calm. The day before the tribunal was to hand down its decision there was a bomb attack on the offices of the BRB, the Brigade for the Repression of Banditry, on the Quai de Gesvres in Paris, leaving one dead and several wounded. In your opinion, was there any connection with the Abdallah affair?

J.P.M. I don't think so. On the contrary, that attack could only do Georges a disservice by trying to influence the police and the authorities. It was a challenge to the state, as Charles Pasqua, the Interior Minister, stated the next day, and I cannot imagine the French government simply obeying that sort of order. Of course, some journalists suggested it was the FARL's doing, but those suggestions were not taken seriously by investigators. Two days later, Action Directe claimed responsibility for the act. Their responsibility still has not been established, since an analysis of the explosive device pointed the police toward an Armenian terrorist group.

In the eyes of the general public, for whom all terrorists are often lumped together, it is useless to make distinctions among various groups. But since coming to know 'Alex', I have had proof that he had no connection with Action Directe, and he never mentioned the Armenians to me. There remains the theory of a 'great clandestine leader' who pulls the strings, using each of the terrorist groups in turn. But that is another story.

On July 10th, the day after the attack against the BRB, and a few hours before the verdict was to be delivered, I went to see Abdallah. For the first time, he appeared extremely dejected and down in the dumps. Commenting on the attack that had occurred the day before, he said that it couldn't have come at a worse time. He regretted that he had expressed himself so badly in court the week before, or at least not as well as he might have liked. The regrets of a revolutionary who knows he is about to be silenced? Or a defendant's disappointment that he had been unable to convince his judges? If that was the case it would be sweet revenge for the legal system since Abdallah, after having denied during the trial that it could be independent, now regretted that his appearance before the tribunal had not gone better.

Georges insisted he would not appeal against the decision, no matter what the sentence might be. 'The French government must take its responsibilities,' he said. I did not argue with his decision. As a lawyer, I was there to counsel him; as a militant, I followed orders. As for the Service, it was awaiting the sentence in order to be able to re-evaluate the situation.

L.G. The Lyons court sentenced Abdallah to four years in prison. How did he react?

J.P.M. In the courtroom he remained stone-faced. He was dressed, perhaps symbolically, in a three-piece black suit, almost mourning clothes. That afternoon I went back to see him at the prison. 'I hope, for France's sake, I'll be set free before the end of August. If I'm not, the country will become uninhabitable. It won't just be one Metro train that's stopped, but all traffic,' he announced, sounding almost regretful.

Having received a four-year prison sentence, Abdallah could expect what is called 'rapid conditional release', if the Justice Minister agreed to it. He had already served practically the minimum time in prison to make him eligible for this special treatment. There would be a delay, a month or two, but no more than that. In order to be freed, once his conditional release was signed, Abdallah would still have to obtain a dismissal of the Paris case which was then in preparation.

Secondly, Abdallah had explicitly set a time limit for his release: before the end of August. Was he saying it to me, or to the microphones in the prison visitors' room? It is probable that this information was transmitted two ways, and I reported his statements to the Service, who interpreted them as an ultimatum. Abdallah's threats were clear: 'France will become uninhabitable,' could only mean that our country would be living under a constant threat of bombings everywhere.

Abdallah was not only talking about Paris, although his allusions to the Metro subway were clear. We must remember that by the beginning of 1986, even though Paris had already suffered a series of bombings, the most serious one, according to the police, had been miraculously foiled when a Metro passenger spotted a suspicious package under a train seat, threw it out of the window near the Châtelet-Les Halles Metro station, and then set off an alarm. Very few details were made public, but the police did announce that there might have been a real massacre if the package-bomb had exploded. There, too, according to the Service, Abdallah was not merely making idle conversation.

L.G. Was Abdallah actually calling for murders to be committed?

J.P.M. You can read it that way. One can also interpret it as a prisoner's opinion, while speaking to his lawyer under the seal of lawyer/client privilege, indicating that his comrades might lose patience and set off a certain type of operation over which he no longer had control or influence, nor about which he would have advance knowledge. That statement got me moving, and the Service even more than me. Especially since Georges had suddenly expressed a completely new philosophy of terrorist action. 'There are no longer "clean" or "dirty" targets,' he said to me. 'The whole of France is responsible. There has been no revolutionary, nor Arab, solidarity in respect of my case. Everyone is happily wallowing in the imperialist feast, even those who only pick up its crumbs. Now the FARL will strike, and their firepower is quite another thing to the CSPPA's.'

I had the impression that afternoon that Georges had lost his temper and been carried away. He alone could not have decided on this new theory of 'everyone is responsible'. I also had the feeling that he was making reference to some recent news of his comrades, received through some particular channel. But that theory, as revolting as it was, was in line with the FARL's logic: individual, or foreign, targets in the centre of Paris at the beginning of 1982; mass, although not murderous, attacks up until the Point-Show bombing at the start of 1986. But now? After the Lyons verdict, the group was going to try to strike hard and to hurt innocent people, so as to oblige the government to bow to pressure by terrorizing public opinion.

For the first time Abdallah had named the FARL as the group that was going to carry out the attack. He talked about them as if they were strangers, and not at all as if he was still leading them from inside prison. Could Abdallah have curbed his comrades' strategy? The Service didn't think so, since he appeared disillusioned. His allusions to the lack of 'revolutionary' solidarity, as well as to the disinterest of Arab immigrants living in France, proved it. By 'revolutionaries' might he have meant Action Directe, for example? That would be support for the theory according to which the FARL had no connections with, and more or less resented, the people of Action Directe. Long before the Lyons trial, for example, Abdallah had told me that Hamami had 'largely disappointed us . . .'

As to the lack of solidarity among Arab immigrants, Georges' statement quite puzzled the Service. If it was true, what about the CSPPA? Did Abdallah mean that the militants operating in Paris at the start of 1986 were foreigners who had come to France for the occasion?

L.G. The most important thing is Abdallah's mention of the FARL's 'firepower'. What did you know about that?

J.P.M. Not very much. His threats were clear; I reported them, and the visitors' room walls had ears. But after the Lyons verdict

Abdallah was placed in total isolation, could no longer talk to other prisoners, or receive mail. All he knew about the situation was what was reported in the newspapers and on the radio. This isolation measure, which the Service had hoped for, had perhaps been decided by the judge or the police, but it definitely pleased the *Piscine*. If Abdallah wanted to send information out, I would have to be his messenger.

Unhappily, that measure would prove ineffective. Ever since the Lyons verdict, whether due to a lack of trust, or because he could no longer intervene, Georges had given me no further assignments, except for requests regarding his personal linen. I was still under strict orders not to try offering him broad hints, by asking for news of 'Nathalie', for example. As time passed the only thing I could do was tell him that I felt the noose tightening around my own neck, and would soon need a fall-back position. But in vain. I would broach the subject every time I came into the visitors' room, saying: 'So, what's the news?' 'News?' he would say, 'but it's up to you to give it to me. You know they're keeping me in total isolation.'

I had no idea, obviously, how to locate the FARL's firepower, but I had very few doubts with regard to the group's resources. The episode during which Georges had given me responsibility for moving the 'strategic material', in 1984, was still fresh in my memory. A perusal of the Italian and French indictments proved – if the information contained in them was correct – that the FARL had numerous safe houses and hideouts in France, and in other European countries.

L.G. How useful were you, before and during the September 1986 bombings?

J.P.M. Not at all, I fear, and it made me seethe with anger. Abdallah had set a time limit: the end of August. The Service had become a hive of activity, but if it was gathering intelligence, the information was not coming from me since Georges had told me nothing of importance since his comments directly after the verdict. And 'they' were not keeping me informed about the Service's activities . . . 'They' had simply ordered me not to break off contact with Georges in case he might want to use me as a messenger again. I believe the Service did not have enough information to permit them to act. For example, in September 1986, I had a meeting with my handler in a cafe on Paris's Rue de Rennes, approximately one hundred metres from the Tati discount store, and less than an hour before the most murderous of the bombings. Even Frédéric Oriach, my other lead in the case, had not been in touch with me since his return from Syria, early in September. I was cut off.

L.G. What was Abdallah's reaction to the American involvement in this case, and the fact that Washington had protested the light sentence and then entered the Paris case as *'partie civile'*?*

J.P.M. Abdallah repeated to me what he had said to Gilles Boulouque, the examining magistrate, when told that the United States had entered the case. He took it as 'a true act of war' by the Americans against his country, and demanded that France choose between 'the case, or pleasing the Americans'. He even made an appeal to French sovereignty, whereas for months he had been denying it existed, accusing Paris of automatically ranging itself in 'the imperialist camp'.

I think the American involvement, which was an embarrassment to the French government, was the last straw and determined the FARL's strategy. All moderation, all prudence that might have remained, in expectation of an eventual act of clemency, or a compromise with the French authorities, became useless as any possibility of Abdallah being released was now fading. By entering his case, the greatest power on earth was sending a signal that it did not intend to let him slip through its fingers.

Perhaps it was then that Abdallah's comrades conceived of the September bombings as a retaliation against what Abdallah had denounced as the American 'act of war'. And it would take place on France's territory, since it was there that Washington had chosen to fight. There would be terrible consequences for the Parisians, but the Lebanese extremists', or Palestinian militants'

---

* In the French legal system, an injured party, called the *'partie civile'*, whose interests are not identical to those of the prosecution, may also be represented at a trial.

¹ogic could be analyzed as follows: they would be fighting almost openly against France and the United States, with no other goal than to spread terror and violence since, after the series of bombings in September, Georges no longer believed there was any possibility of his release.

L.G. The bombings began on September 4th, when a large quantity of explosives failed to go off in an RER train* at the Gare de Lyon. That matches up almost too well with Abdallah's prediction.

J.P.M. If you are trying to make me say that Georges knew all about it, or that I invented his Lyons statements after the fact, that's on your own responsibility. The failed bombing had been preceded by a warning from the CSPPA, sent from Beirut on September 1st, reminding the world of the ultimatum that had been launched from the prison visitors' room in Lyons. The strange thing is, if from that point on the FARL intended to fight in the open, why did they not claim responsibility for the Paris bombings directly, instead of allowing the CSPPA to do so as they had at the beginning of the year? It might be understandable as regards the 'failed' bombing at the Gare de Lyon, since the FARL insisted that all its actions be a success. But it was less understandable later, from the attack on the Hôtel de Ville post office to the one on the Rue de Rennes.

I am not convinced that the 'failed' bombing of the RER train was truly a 'failure', but that it was intended, rather, as a last warning. The police were fairly close-mouthed in their statements to the press. Imagine if the bombing had succeeded: at least one hundred people would have been killed, according to investigators. And who would risk travelling on the Metro afterwards? Considering the potential number of victims, there would be no reason for more bombings. On the contrary, from the Hôtel de Ville post office to the Casino shopping centre cafeteria at La Défense, to the Rue de Rennes, the terrorists maintained a steady progression both of horror, and of the number of victims.

* RER Express Metro system, serving the nearby suburbs of Paris.

L.G. The CSPPA demands were the same as they had been the preceding spring. They still demanded the release of Abdallah, and the Armenian, Garabejian, as well as Anis Naccache. Do you still believe this was a decoy, and that their real objective was Abdallah?

J.P.M. The CSPPA had increased its demands. Besides the release of the three, the organization was now demanding in its communiqués a radical change in France's Near-East policies, most notably the withdrawal of the multinational forces in Southern Lebanon, for which France was providing the bulk of the troops. I can't say if the two items are connected, but in the same month as the Paris bombings there were several attacks against the UN troops, with a large number of dead and wounded. Abdallah had talked to me about it during my visits. Although he had not made precise threats, he had been hoping for some time that all French, and especially their UN troops, would pull out of Lebanon.

I don't know if it was the FARL who carried out the September bombings, or if it only gave logistical help to the people who had been signing their terrorist activities 'CSPPA' ever since the beginning of the year. The police theory by which all possible leads to the authors of those crimes came down to Abdallah's friends, and brothers, seems shortsighted to me. Abdallah never talked to me about his brothers, and the press conferences they held in northern Lebanon made whoever suggested that trail look ridiculous.*

That whole period was very hard on me. I was not the only one, but I had specific reasons for thinking I had failed in the mission I had set myself. Each time I went to see Georges after a bombing, he would gratify me with a 'no comment', and assure me that he disapproved of the methods being used. But he did not want me to declare it publicly, and as of the beginning of September even forbade me all contact with the press.

Did those murderous acts serve his ends? I don't think so. If

* Maurice and Robert Abdallah, Abdallah's brothers, were each accused of the bomb attacks by the French police. They both held press conferences in Lebanon to declare their innocence.

144

Abdallah appeared depressed after the Lyons verdict; he was even more so after receiving the visit (to which many objected) of Monsignor Hilarion Capucci, the Lebanese Orthodox Patriarch. That visit by a progressivist prelate, known for his ties with the Palestinians, set off a controversy in France. For my part, I can only repeat what a journalist reported. Albin Chalandon, the Justice Minister, was extremely upset when the ultrasensitive microphones placed in the prison's visitors' room did not manage to record the 'extremely Christian' conversation, as the Monsignor would later describe it, that followed after he murmured who-knows-what in Abdallah's ear. Georges never told me exactly what had been said, but he seemed worried and pessimistic, remaining absolutely mute on the subject, as if someone very high up had abandoned him.

L.G. Before authorizing that visit, the French authorities seemed to be trying to make Abdallah crack. Alain Marsaud, the examining magistrate responsible for dealing with those bombings, came to the prison to question Abdallah as a witness . . .

J.P.M. As far as I know, it was the first time that rather strange procedure had been used since the time of the Algerian War. Since he had been kept in isolation, Abdallah could not have been a witness to anything. Judge Marsaud, who has since been promoted to the position of prosecutor for the judicial department specializing in the fight against terrorism, also ordered that Abdallah's cell in the Santé Prison be searched. He was operating within the guidelines of the investigation that had begun hard on the heels of the bombing at the Motor Vehicle Office at the Paris Prefecture of Police, another terrorist challenge directed against the investigators, flouting them in their own territory. I learned of the judge's initiative because on the same day, on the Service's orders, I was to visit Abdallah in order to test his reactions.

Then my orders were countermanded. I was to wait until the next day to see Georges. The conclusions I drew from that made me smile: the *Piscine* had seen through the judge's initiatives. When I saw Georges he calmly described his meeting with the magistrate. Of course, the search had turned up nothing, since the police had taken nothing away for closer examination, but Georges had been made to take an X-ray just in case he might have swallowed some compromising document. He was held under close guard in his cell for four days in all, while various policemen interrogated him in relays in vain. Georges told me, but I found this incredible, that the judge had made death threats against him, telling him he was going to be killed within the next forty-eight hours. This was so outrageous that I didn't even challenge his statement but began to doubt everything he had said. He himself admitted he was losing his memory, and that he often flew into a rage at the conditions in which he was being held, and which he found hard to endure. This may prove a consolation to those people who think democracies are too lenient. No one takes imprisonment easily.

L.G. At a time when Paris was being drenched in blood, wasn't Abdallah displaying a propensity to play the martyr?

J.P.M. I'm not sure that the toll of victims in the Rue de Rennes bombing, murderous as it was, kept him from sleeping. Georges is Lebanese, and for more than ten years had lived through his own country's tragedy, with the periodic bombings which were infinitely more bloody than those committed in Paris that September. According to his own logic, it was not a list of French dead and wounded that could move him.

On the other hand he was aware that it was a national tragedy for us, and that the bombings were giving rise to extremely hostile feelings toward him. Did he exaggerate them, fantasizing about his own importance? Was he compensating for his lost liberty, which now had been definitively delayed by the clearly expressed will of the government? Did he see himself as a heroic figure, elevate himself to the status of martyr? Surely there was some of all that in his attitude, which had never been other than that of a prisoner who is as famous as he is despised and isolated. Keeping matters in perspective, I had the impression he had settled into his imprisonment as an internationally known political prisoner . . .

'After all,' he said, 'prison is a part of every militant revolutionary's path . . .'

. . . but also as a forgotten soldier, or a leader who has been sacrificed by his own people.

|12|
THE BREAKING POINT

Shocked by the new wave of bombings, and apparently powerless to do anything to prevent them, Jean-Paul Mazurier found his position more and more untenable. He no longer had Abdallah's confidence, his reason for joining the DGSE was gone. He decided to break with both the terrorists and the Service.

Jean-Paul Mazurier 'Antoine' told me of the bombing massacre on the Rue de Rennes over the telephone. I was in my office, shuffling papers and waiting by the phone as I did every night, in case the 'comrades' should call. The 'comrades'! The word made me sick. There was no television set in the office and I had not turned on the raido. 'Antoine's' announcement of the death toll was horrible: women, children, legs blown away, a Paris pavement transformed into an emergency operating room. On the boulevard outside my window, the emergency-service ambulance sirens were a better indication of the extent of the damage than any news bulletin could be. I was prostrated, my shoulder had locked, I was having trouble breathing, and there was a pain in my chest. And to think there were actually people who believed I sipped champagne or rubbed my hands over every bombing! Paralyzed, unable to think, I telephoned my psychiatrist.

'Doctor, it's me,' I said. 'There's been a bombing on Rue de Rennes, an absolute slaughterhouse. I'm at the end of my tether, I'm having an attack of angina . . .'

'Come to my office,' he said. 'I don't have any more patients today. I'll see you when you get here.'

'No, it's impossible,' I said. 'I still have work to do, and I'm expecting a client.'

The doctor knew nothing about my work as an agent, but he knew I was Abdallah's defence lawyer. I could not tell him the terrorists might be contacting me that evening, wanting me to deliver some message or other. And I would have to control my voice when I talked to them! The doctor advised me to take my daily dose of tranquillizers. I took more than he prescribed, as I had for weeks now, knowing it would have absolutely no effect on me. And the sleeping pills were no longer working, either.

Laurent Gally Did you have those psychosomatic symptoms after every bombing? Did you have them during the first wave of bombings in February-March 1986, when the CSPPA claimed responsibility?

J.P.M. No, or at least not to the same extent. But I was totally revolted by the carnage on the Rue de Rennes. Before that, at each bombing, whether successful or not, as in the failures in the Metro, I would try to learn if there were any victims. The bombings in the winter of 1985 had caused no deaths, except for the Point-Show explosion. Maybe it's terrible to say this, but the fact that the Lebanese terrorist who died in that bombing was, according to investigators, a FARL sympathizer apparently served to calm the public.

I would rate every attack on a scale of seriousness according to the target, the place, the circumstances, and the toll of victims. I continued watching that barometer of terrorism, watching the mercury fall and the weather turn stormy. Because I was thinking rationally, it meant I was still in control of myself. My anxiety was growing, but each time I would put off that final moment when I would be called on to pay. The bombs seemed like warnings, bloody warnings, but warnings just the same. But the carnage in front of the Tati store was the breaking point.

L.G. Was it the Rue de Rennes bombing that made you decide to talk?

J.P.M. No; I had been thinking about it for almost a year, since before the bombings at the end of 1985, but from another point of view. My own lassitude, my disgust, my determination to throw a spanner in the works; there was no lack of excuses. I wanted out, but I wanted to slip away quietly. I had considered writing a novel about how I had become close to the FARL, starting with the ill-starred love between a lawyer-agent and an Arab girl-terrorist serving a long prison sentence in a neighbouring country. The plot was too obvious: everyone would have recognized Joséphine Abdo. But I needed 'them' to recognize me. I wanted everyone concerned – the bar, the Service – to understand that I was 'burning' myself, and to believe I was doing it out of clumsiness, or else literary ambition. I never succeeded in writing one word of that novel.

The situation has changed radically since September. Now I want everything out in the open, with no embellishments even if that means this book will be drier and colder. Because I couldn't stand myself any more, still less my situation, and I wanted to confide in someone. In you, who had been covering the Abdallah affair from the very beginning. Which meant you would be able to challenge me every time I was tempted to lie or, rather, each time I was tempted to embroider what I had done. Your role would be to note the improbabilities, the contradictions, to compare my version with your own information. Even if the improbable – and I'm now thinking of my meeting with the Syrian diplomats, before my trip to Damascus – is a daily part of an agent's life.

L.G. So much for the method you chose. But why the sudden breaking point? Why tell everything now?

J.P.M. Impotence drives you mad. I had been feeling useless for months as, apart from his threats, Abdallah had given me no useful information since the Lyons verdict. The Tati store bombing was the breaking point. It was not only a sign that everything I had tried to do over the last two years had failed, but the seriousness of the bombing rendered any further action futile in advance. Why should I carry even one more message? What for? The group had made up its mind to kill, at random, as many people as possible. There might be another bombing the next day, or a month from now. Abdallah was no longer in control of his comrades.

And then the brutality of the bombing demanded that I break off relations with those people, as I had in 1982. Even for duty's sake, I was no longer able to continue my flirtation with the methods, or theories, of terrorists.

L.G. Nevertheless, you were still seeing Abdallah in the meantime. Why, if you intended to break with him and his group?

J.P.M. I will no longer be an agent when this book is published. But for the moment, I still am, and I obey my orders, which are to maintain contact with Abdallah. But I procrastinate, since I have waited a month and a half to return to see him where previously I saw him at least once a week. Paradoxically, although I have no wish to see Abdallah, I don't hate him. To my mind he is still the leader of the FARL, but the fact he is a prisoner, being held in strict isolation, and that in reality his hands must be clean as regards the latest wave of bombings, does ease my mind. I have always felt a certain respect for him, and believe him to be sincerely motivated. I simply prefer to know that he is in prison rather than to worry about him throwing a bomb, or ordering one to be thrown on some pavement, somewhere. Writing about the revolutionary, Saint-Just, André Malraux said: 'He is pure and cruel at the same time.' I am not Malraux; Abdallah is not Saint-Just, yet that definition does apply to him.

L.G. Nevertheless, those visits do keep you connected with terrorism. There may have been a break, but no real separation. And if tomorrow, or a week from now, you come across some information that might be of immediate use, what would you do with it?

J.P.M. I'd report it, partly out of duty, partly out of habit. But there is no question of my going fishing for information, or subordinating my life to it. Quite simply, I have become incapable of doing it, my enthusiasm is gone, and I have lost my resilience. I want to put an end to an untenable situation.

First of all, there is the matter of how other people see me. When a neighbour of mine, Jean-Edern Hallier, shouts across a cafe at me: 'All those bombings: it's your fault!' I think he's a fool, but the accusation stings like a whip. My colleagues give me the cold shoulder, not as Abdallah's lawyer – even though some openly reproach me for that, as if deep inside itself, democracy would deny an alleged terrorist any defence at all – but for my public utterances. And, after having so often adopted others' opinions as my own, both the Service's, and Abdallah's, I have reached a point where I wonder who I am. I want to find myself again. The only thing of which I am sure is that I still hate the methods and violence of terrorists.

L.G. You told me that since the wave of bombings in September, the police have been treating you like a suspect.

J.P.M. The police have regarded me with a jaundiced eye for a long time now, ever since the beginning of the affair. I think I was under surveillance by Mossad and the DST in 1984, and I'm not sure that part of the *Piscine* doesn't consider me a terrorist lawyer. What *has* changed since September, due to the authorities' growing nervousness and irritability, is that now my office and home are bugged. 'They' told me so. It's not authorized: bugging a lawyer is still illegal when it touches upon lawyer-client privilege. At the time Abdallah was visited by Monsignor Capucci, one of the Santé Prison wardens told me that I had been 'trailing people behind me' for months now, and that he had even been questioned by his superiors, on DST orders, about his relations with me.

Those suspicions did not hasten the decision to remove myself from the affair. It's still rather amusing to have meetings with the Service under the very nose of Police Intelligence, or the DST. The different agencies have been playing games of hide-and-seek amongst themselves in underground car parks, from cafe to cafe, on Paris streets, in unmarked cars, and so on.

L.G. Was it difficult for you to betray your various clients? Do you want to put an end to that, too?

J.P.M. Of course. Over the last two years I was seeing my 'revolutionary' clients only to extract information from them, since an agent obeys orders, and morality never enters into the workings of intelligence agencies. For two years, I struggled with that dilemma. Does the idea that one may save lives justify abusing people's trust? And isn't it worse when you are a lawyer, a prisoner's only hope no matter what his crimes, and he has a right to counsel and to be heard even though society is set against him? Systematically, I had to ignore lawyer-client privilege. It was not easy. At the beginning of Abdallah's imprisonment, when I went to see him and he dictated messages to me, I was supposed to make an oral, later a written, report to the Service. If I waited a few days before writing it up, I would forget two-thirds of the details. It was too heavy a burden on me, and I think my memory unconsciously shied at putting anything in writing.

Today, I fear neither the wrath of the bar council, nor of the justice system. The authorities would find it very difficult to give me a fair trial, since the penal code exempts from prosecution any agent acting on orders of the state. Of course, the Service would have to 'cover' me, but I don't expect they will. No, what is important to me is the average person's opinions. Which means, in the last analysis, my own. I want to be able to look at myself in the mirror in the morning, to have a clear image of myself, one which is no longer a reflection of a series of masks.

L.G. How many did you wear?

J.P.M. There was the mask of the revolutionary. I played that part rather badly, but it served its purpose. I feel no pain tearing that one away, but it will not change one iota my opinion about the justice of certain causes, notably the fate of the Palestinians. There was also the mask of the lawyer. The profession had a real hold on me, and I think I exercised it to the best of my ability against the judicial authorities, including in the interests of my clients who were alleged to be members of the FARL. What I can no longer bear, and what is obliging me to leave my profession, is the fact that at each of my prison visits I consciously lied to people against whom I was fighting, but whom I respect. I felt affection for Abdo, a certain admiration for Abdallah, pity for Mansuri, and an almost instinctive camaraderie with Carette. I'll say nothing about Oriach, as my personal relations with him were very difficult.

And then there is the profession of agent. I sacrificed everything, too much, to it. With no results. I voluntarily went into the profession, was excited when I uncovered my first piece of intelligence at the end of 1984. It finally reached the point where I was thinking of my contacts almost as family. First of all, because my activities were wreaking havoc with my attempts to lead a normal private life, but also because my normal clientele had been reduced to nothing, and I found myself driven either to continue performing a routine in which I was now feeling useless, or breaking with it, and doing so openly.

And, finally, there is the question of my own life, and trying to regain some control over it. I don't want to hate myself any longer, to despise myself, or keep running away, still dragging behind me I don't know what sort of reputation as an alcoholic, or a drug addict. If there had been another way out, which would have allowed me some peace, I would not have launched myself into these disclosures. After all, it is me, more than Abdallah, whom readers will be judging.

L.G. Do you believe your story of the Abdallah affair will serve the cause of justice?

J.P.M. I never even considered making accusations against Abdallah, and nothing I say here can help the prosecution's case. Perhaps they will try to force me to testify, to tell what I know. I have no proof of what I have said here, and it will be easy for them to accuse me of megalomania. When I joined the Service, I had a vision of my role as being strictly preventive, not repressive. There can be no thought of releasing Abdallah's lawyer (which I have been since 1984, and still am) from the seal of secrecy of the lawyer-client relationship, in order to lend further weight to the charges.

On the other hand, I suppose Georges' comrades, and Oriach's, as well as some others, will take this book seriously, and will gnash their teeth. But somehow I can't see myself asking for police protection.

And, finally, there is the Service. I am disengaging myself from it, but I am not betraying it. I still agree with its objectives, if not always with its methods. Did I sign up with the Service for life? No, and no matter what anyone says, in the Faust myth it is Mephistopheles who offers the contract. The Service is not the devil: any action taken against me, including the obvious 'hit-and-run' accident which every agent being hired hears described as a final possibility, would only prove the opposite. What I engaged to do, what I am holding to, and what I will respect, is my silence regarding the essentials. May they forget me as I, too, want to forget.

L.G. The Service has another, more traditional, solution: an agent may ask to be put on the inactive list.

J.P.M. No, it's the contrary that happens: from time to time the Service's plans may include putting an agent in 'cold storage'. 'They' were planning to do that with me at the end of October, since I was at the end of my tether, and falling apart physically. But, more important, I was of no more use to them since neither Oriach nor Carette nor Abdallah had given me the least bit of useful information in the prior four months. Then suddenly the Service decided to reactivate me, asking me to take up my infernal round of prison visits in search of information.

But no matter what happened I would never accept being put in 'cold storage'. It is not immodesty on my part, but either they kept me operational, as I had been during the long months since 1984, taking part to the best of my ability in the fight against terrorism, or I would leave the Service. Both because, without having wanted it, I was of no further use and because I have no desire to be a 'black agent' for ever. And I am fed up with my mask, or masks.

L.G. There is another possibility you have never mentioned. You may have been 'burned'.

J.P.M. I considered that possibility. Abdallah had been suspicious of me before he asked me to move the weapons, in the summer of 1984, because he suspected me of having my own revolutionary goals. But after questioning me over a long period of time, he seemed satisfied. The second time, on my return from Belgrade at the end of November 1984, he asked his comrades to investigate me, but without saying anything to me about it. 'The Blond' had disappeared; militants had been arrested in Italy, and so on. That investigation, which I knew nothing about, ended in August 1985 with the dismissal of all charges. I was not a traitor; merely careless. Abdallah scolded me for my blunders, my flightiness, my lack of vigilance, as if he had at last noticed that I had absolutely no training as a militant.

I have certainly had no further information since July, but if Abdallah suspected me of being an agent, why didn't he send me off on wild goose chases that would upset the Service's plans and divert it from its objectives, and which his comrades could easily have overseen? On the contrary, Abdallah's last message, which was meant as much for the microphones in the walls as for me, was a warning that France would become uninhabitable. Although that was an exaggeration, it was not disinformation. September 1986 proved that.

Abdallah had worried about my safety for two years; why should he suspect me now? That was always one of his favourite subjects of conversation. 'Christmas is coming,' he said one day, with a wink, 'I hope you won't be doing your Christmas shopping in a department store . . . your office is the only safe place in Paris.' The joke was in questionable taste, but the intention behind it was rather nice.

Another indication: for two weeks running after the September bombings, a popular French magazine published what purported to be revelations about the FARL. In the first issue I was listed as one of the group's sympathizers, if not an accomplice. By the following week, I had become a DST informer! Warned in advance, Abdallah asked me to bring him both issues. He read them and, about my contradictory position said: 'What's wrong with these people, always getting on your back?' He smiled: 'The cops are giving out conflicting stories to the press. I hope the comrades won't be fooled by this disinformation.'

And finally, I don't believe Abdallah would have been able to control himself during our meetings in the visitors' room if he thought I was an agent. Since the time he was put in isolation, he had had time to rethink the entire affair, almost day by day. And in that case, seeing me would simply be a waste of time. But why? Despite everything that separated us, did he still have some feelings of attachment towards me? I'm tempted to find out. I want to see him one last time, and tell him everything. Face to face. That would be the only truly courageous act I would consider I have accomplished in the last two years. And it would be very difficult for me. I do not fear a physical attack, but I do fear his contempt, the possibility that he might turn away without a word, without a glance, and return to his cell, leaving me even more alone than he is.

L.G. If Abdallah reads this book, would he find in it any justification for your actions?

J.P.M. I doubt it. But he ought to concentrate on self-criticism, even though he already spends much of his time in that sort of exercise: after all, it was he who time and again came to me. Like me, he lacked prudence and acumen, although I do have admiration for his intellectual capacities. There remains the inexplicable, that I inspire confidence. I do not forget that, in his first months of detention, Abdallah had no one but me at his side. So, there was a sort of obligatory trust. Betraying him cost me an enormous physical and psychological effort. I had to act naturally, speak in a composed manner, although every time I left the prison I would be shivering and ice-cold, and I would sometimes throw up with the feeling that I was vomiting up my own self.

Today, I believe the sympathy, esteem and affinity we felt for each other will never disappear. Each of us, on his own side, was fighting for an opposing cause. I cheated. That cannot erase the rest, I hope.

There remain the 'others'. I don't give a damn about Oriach's opinion, which doesn't mean that I'm not afraid of his personal reaction. As for Carette, I imagine that he will laugh. He's a good sport, with a good-natured mentality. He always took complete responsibility for himself as leader of the CCC and never provided me with any major information. No doubt he will draw the conclusion from this affair that one must never trust anyone, which during the time of its earliest activities in Belguim was his group's golden rule. What makes me uneasy is the predictable disgust and sadness of Joséphine Abdo's reaction. I consider her as innocent, I abused her trust, and I still have great affection for her.

|13| THE FARL

Following his decision to withdraw from the Abdallah case, Jean-Paul Mazurier talks about the background to the affair. He discusses the part played by the French and other intelligence agencies, the relationship of the FARL to other terrorist groups and to the countries which support them, and Abdallah's own position in the hierarchy of international terrorism.

Jean-Paul Mazurier My story is finished, or almost. Since the September bombings I have been no more than a shadowy figure in the Abdallah case. Still present, but only in half-tints. The affair has become international, my client's fate now linked to all kinds of diplomatic imperatives, as well as to domestic politics. The government took the case in hand, and so much the better. It should have happened sooner, considering all the information the authorities had at their disposal. It was obvious, since the end of 1984, that this explosive case could only degenerate into something worse as its details became public.

Laurent Gally Did Abdallah calculate that the government's attitude towards his case would depend, in part, on which political party was in power?

J.P.M. He never spoke to me of any particular political personality. When he was convicted, he hoped that his case would be quickly settled, according to an agreement the government must have known about, I think. But Abdallah considered the Socialists to be particularly pro-Zionist, and when Jacques Chirac took office as prime minister, the Point-Show bombing dramatically revived the case, as if the group intended to demonstrate that it knew who was in power, and that our government leaders' political tone mattered little to them.

L.G. Do you believe that all the information you uncovered was systematically transmitted to the proper people, at the political level?

J.P.M. I'm not sure. For example, I was taken to task for the bluntly alarmist terms I employed in my France-Inter radio interview last February. The Service had told me to hammer it home, but by prophesying that other, more murderous bombings were sure to occur I wanted to alert the authorities, as well as public opinion.

I don't know how my information has been passed on since I became involved in this case. I did continue my occasional contacts with the investigating magistrate who helped me at the beginning, but I have not seen him since early in 1986. I was not reporting to him, but I was informing him, in general terms, of the leads that were taking shape. Apart from that particular channel, everything I learned was transmitted only by the *Piscine*, and my handler or my immediate supervisor there. In principle, all information should have been transmitted to the Defence Ministry, to which the Service is subject. As for it having gone any higher, I mean the probability of it having reached the Prime Minister at the Matignon Palace, or the President of the Republic at the Elysée Palace, I do not know.

But since the end of 1985 the number of ministries involved in the Abdallah case has multiplied: Justice, Interior, Foreign Affairs, and Defence. Those ministers, by the way, are all members of the Internal Security Council, which has debated the affair several times. Each minister had his own sources of information: for the Justice Ministry, the investigation dossiers; the DST for Interior; *Piscine* reports for Defence; and so on. And the Prime Minister's own services had to sum up and synthesize it all.

At the Service's behest, I also spoke several times by telephone to someone who introduced himself as the 'authority'. I am unable to define, or describe, this person's position within the government.

This must all seem very vague. To make sense of it one can take the most optimistic appraisal possible: that the totality of information gathered served to guarantee that all political decisions taken were based on the full facts. Unfortunately, there is also another possibility: that the Service and the DST do not co-operate with each other, but quite the opposite. And this opposition is painfully obvious from the very beginning of the affair and right through the case, at the time of Abdallah's arrest in Lyons or during Peyroles' release, for example.

L.G. When there are conflicting theories, the best-supported one must prevail. From the very beginning, didn't the DST have more information about the case than the *Piscine*?

J.P.M. We would have to learn exactly what the DST knew. What is certain, is that at the beginning the *Piscine* launched itself into the case on very little evidence since they had no photographs, and no idea of Abdallah's identity, as I later learned. Throughout those years the DST seemed to be keeping several lengths ahead: the search and discovery of a weapons cache at the Rue Lacroix hideout testifies to that.

I have no concrete explanation for the rivalry which, it seems, is a long-standing one between two agencies who should have been co-operating with each other on this case. On the other hand, while reading the court records I was struck by the agreement of information and evidence in them, in Italy as well as in France. The entire history of the FARL from about 1980 is retraced there, with a list of various European safe houses and hideouts not only in France and Italy but also in Spain and in Switzerland, where the hideouts take the form of bank accounts! This information cannot be attributed to the *Piscine*, nor to the DST, nor to their Italian colleagues. This fund of common knowledge must be a police translation of an extremely detailed report compiled by Mossad, the Israeli intelligence service. The Italian dossier formally acknowledges the source, and the former director of the DST refers to it in his report on the Peyroles affair.

L.G. If identical information is systematically accepted by several countries as the basis for court cases, isn't there a risk of disinformation?

J.P.M. Certainly, but in this affair Israeli-Western solidarity was not just a catch phrase. Abdallah denounced it constantly, and considered the State of Israel as his real enemy, so much so that he literally cannot distinguish between a Jew and a Zionist. According to him, when a Jew says he is anti-Zionist it is a political aberration. He once told me that he refused to talk to a Jewish prisoner walking beside him in the exercise yard. Abdallah is convinced that war between Jews and Arabs is not only inevitable but desirable, and that it goes on constantly, if only in a latent form. If he does not talk about the destruction of the Jews as a people, he does openly desire the destruction of Israel as a state. Inversely, it is only natural that Mossad closely follows the political evolution of the FARL, and its more militant members' peregrinations throughout Europe. Apparently, however, Mossad did not follow them to the very end, since it too did not deter the September bombings.

Israeli intelligence has probably been on Georges' trail since 1976, as they suspect him of being an accomplice in, if not the author of, the assassination of Francis Melloy, at that time American ambassador to Lebanon. I was always surprised by the apparent naivety of the biographies of Abdallah which appeared in the press. He was always described as being a former teacher who had only become a full-time militant in 1979. Georges never mentioned his past as a teacher to me, but he did admit in my hearing, and this was also established by the Italian courts, that he had contacts with certain members of the Italian Red Brigades in 1976. Not in order to be trained by them, but for him to train them in the use of weapons and explosives. When I saw Abdo in prison after the Rome trial she asked me to re-establish contact with the Red Brigades so that they could organize a common strategy, but without telling me exactly how to go about it. I thought that, what with the CCC, Oriach, etc., it was not up to me to bring together movements which were not already united.

L.G. Are you certain all those movements did not have more organic ties with the FARL?

J.P.M. Absolutely, as a whole series of indications show. When Abdallah came to see me in 1982 he had no idea of how to get in touch with Action Directe. And that situation had barely changed, since a short time after Georges' arrest in Lyons I received a visit from a mysterious stranger – I shall say no more about him other than that he was not a member of the rank and file – who, in the name of Action Directe, wanted to meet Abdallah so as to establish a connection between the two groups. I relayed this offer to Georges after first having informed the Service. The *Piscine* was extremely disappointed when Abdallah categorically rejected the proposition. Also, Georges, who liked Mohand Hamami, would later confess his disappointment in him.

Putting to one side the very special case of Frédéric Oriach, I can only remind you of Carette's hostility to the FARL, to the point that he judged the Paris bombings of September 1986 'revolting'. Perhaps he has asked that I no longer represent him because he fears any association with FARL terrorism, even by way of his lawyer.

I cannot forget that from the time of our very first meetings Abdallah dreamed of establishing an 'internationalist revolutionary movement'. The operation planned for 15 October 1984 was to have led to the release of militant revolutionaries being held in several countries. Also, Abdallah speaks fluent Arabic, French, Italian, and Spanish. In prison, he asked me to bring him some foreign-language study books, and he is learning German and Turkish. That's quite a lot, especially since he also told Abdo to start learning Spanish. All this effectively delineates Western Europe as an area of operations, even though Abdallah is not very handy in English. And I believe the group might be able to find a sort of fall-back position, or jumping-off place, in Spain. According to the case files, the FARL had safe houses at Alcala de Henares, near Madrid, and Carette once asked me to represent militant members of Spain's GRAPO* who were having legal problems. I did not follow that up, and did not even tell the Service about it. The 'Spanish hypothesis' is not new here: all European intelligence services are familiar with it.

* Extreme-left Spanish group of ultra-Marxist persuasion. Credited with numerous terrorist attacks by the Madrid authorities.

L.G. As the presumed leader of the FARL, how many militants does Abdallah claim to control?

J.P.M. He said nothing to me about that for a very long time. I had heard contradictory reports. He was telling me he controlled all sorts of hideouts in France, but at the same time he was asking me to help him move some weapons. All this changed while he was in custody. Recently, to hear him talk, he has 'thousands' of comrades, either combattants or sympathizers, who are standing behind him in his political aims. In Abdallah's mind, his troops include everyone who organizes the resistance against Israel, and in some way the FARL is to be the spearhead of the Lebanese Resistance.

Experts on the Lebanese situation may not necessarily agree, but it is not up to me to determine the exact outlines of the group. Those outlines can be rather hazy. For Abdallah there was absolutely no question of automatically opposing, for example, the Hezbollah, if the goals of their struggle were the same as his. He spoke to me of the Druzes as possible allies, while claiming that they were extremely dependent on Syria since, according to Abdallah, President Assad and the father of Walid Jumblatt, historical leader of the Druzes, were close rivals . . . until the former physically eliminated the latter. Obviously, I leave all responsibility for that statement to Abdallah. What is certain is that Abdallah hates the Lebanese Phalangists, who are Christian, as is he. He labels them all 'fascists', and in March 1985 was dreading he might fall into their hands if he were expelled from France. That possibility arose with the unfortunate French international rogatory commission in Beirut, which might also have been at the root of the Peyroles affair.

The FARL are always described as the terrorist group responsible for the latest bombings in France, as well as in Italy. But whenever there is an attempt to locate them, geographically, in Lebanon, it is officially limited to seeing them as a particularly close-knit family community, around the villages of Andakat and Kubayat. That is only an approximation. Abdallah claims as his own a number of operations carried out in southern Lebanon, near the Israeli border. To illustrate the inanity of trying to define his group exactly, Abdallah generally cites the Arab proverb: 'My brother and I against my cousin; my brother, cousin and I against the stranger . . .'

L.G. That's not very Marxist. It sounds like a description of feuds among Lebanese clans.

J.P.M. Why should Georges escape the phenomenon that seems to rule the social and political life of his country? His discourse remains extremely Marxist, perhaps due to his education. For example, he denies the worth of all religion, judging it the basic factor dividing his people. But he never talked to me about the rise of Arab religious integrationism, or of the militant Islamic movement of the ayatollahs, or of Hezbollah. Lebanese reality is so variable that Georges himself recognizes that, from where he now sits in prison, he is quite out of his depth. This does not stop there from being a certain Christian tinge to his theories of armed struggle: for years he talked about his targets as being 'clean', or 'dirty', which has a heavy moral connotation.

There is another aspect to Abdallah that has appeared since the Lyons trial. If one can believe what he says, his name, or rather his first name, is now a symbol in northern Lebanon and in West Beirut. And he is now in the slow process of changing his position from one of symbol to that of possible martyr. He has a quasi-Christian vocation for martyrdom, assuring me that prison and death are part of the militant path. He takes strength from that view of things, since he does not handle being imprisoned very well. Even before the Justice Minister said anything about his coming Assizes trial,* Abdallah already saw himself being sentenced to another very long term in prison. But things may still change.

L.G. That position as a symbol, or possible martyr. Does this mean Abdallah is truly one of the heads of the armed struggle in the Near-East?

J.P.M. Certainly. He may be one of the heads of that struggle, but not necessarily the official leader of a revolutionary movement integrated into a larger political entity. This is both his strength

---

* Abdallah's second trial, in Paris, began on 23 February 1987.

and his weakness. Speaking about George Habash, head of the Popular Front for the Liberation of Palestine (of which, some people claim, Abdallah was, or may have been, a cadre), Abdallah said to me that gaining power makes one lose a true revolutionary perspective. He made similarly terse and brutal comments to me about Yasser Arafat's PLO and Abou Abbas' PLF, which was responsible for the hijacking of the Italian cruiseship, *Achille Lauro*. But he never said anything about Abou Nidal, for example, and he certainly does not mean to place himself at the same level in the terrorist hierarchy.

On reflection, I can only compare him to the world-famous terrorist, Carlos. This is not to denigrate him as the 'terrorist' *par excellence*. But according to press reports of the various leaders' respective positions in the unstable world of revolutionary movements, he is at once a leader and a *franc tireur* whose life is totally dedicated to action in the field. A telltale sign? At the time of his arrest, Mansuri was carrying several kilos of explosives in his suitcase, as if the FARL wanted no logistical help from any government.

This might have had consequences for Abdallah. Although he appeared to be controlling his group with an iron hand at the beginning of his imprisonment, it seemed to me that later on Jacqueline Esber had begun displaying tendencies towards independence. And during the September bombings, although Abdallah was perhaps warned of his comrades' overall strategy, he was certainly not given details of the operations in advance.

L.G. His group is being financed by someone. He talked to you primarily about two countries, Syria and Libya, as being able to take him in once he was released. In the light of your experience, is the FARL a dependent of one of these countries?

J.P.M. I know nothing of how his group is financed. Abdallah mentioned several other Arab countries: Algeria, South Yemen, Iran, as well as Syria and Libya. And for a simple reason: he feels that, fundamentally, his struggle has the support of all progressive Arab countries. One could go into details, but my evidence is slender. Everyone knows that he had a real Algerian passport, as well as one issued by Malta. So what conclusion can one draw?

On the other hand, Abdallah did admit to having made a huge mistake during the first interrogation after his arrest, by telling the police his movement was principally based in Syria and Lebanon. Talleyrand wrote: 'Beware of your first reaction; it's generally the right one . . .' As for Lebanon, I'm certain it is the FARL's primary base. There remains Syria, of which much has been said lately, notably after the English provided 'proof' of Damascus' involvement in certain terrorist attacks. Abdallah never disclosed anything to me about this. On the contrary, he displayed a certain wariness towards the Syrians: 'One must not deal with the big animal,' read one of his messages. I can remember the ambiguous meetings I had with the Syrian diplomats before my trip to Damascus. My mission was a total failure, but that did not stop them from keeping in touch with me. Thus, just before I was to leave for the second Trieste trial, I informed them I intended to accompany Abdo and Mansuri to Damascus, if they were freed, and I was granted a second visa.

Quite recently, I saw those diplomats again. Last June, Frédéric Oriach went to the Syrian consulate to ask for a visa, giving my name as reference. I was not told about it, but it worked and Oriach was granted his visa that same day. During the summer, a young German of Indian extraction, who said he was a member of the Red Army Faction and wanted by the police in his own country, made exactly the same request to the Syrian consulate using my name as reference. He was told to present a letter from me as guarantee. So, to my great surprise, the young man came to see me at my office. In an attempt to clear up the matter, I accompanied him to the Syrian consular offices and saw the diplomat who, at our first meeting, had refused me a visa. This time he was effectively asking me for my personal guarantee for the West German militant, which I gave, but what else could I do? He then gave me an overview of the situation.

This diplomat, who made it clear he was at all times acting as a representative of his nation, and was not discussing these matters personally, assured me that Damascus did not consider itself concerned in matters relating to the FARL. If he accepted my guarantee in granting visas it was, he said, out of 'personal friendship', as well as 'out of respect for the struggle I was waging for his Arab brothers'. Behind that wooden language, I could tell that he was distancing himself, as he had done before with my trip to Damascus, from the actions of the FARL, which the press was describing as being remote-controlled by certain officials of the Syrian intelligence services. His mention of my 'struggle' was, to all appearances, contradictory since to whom was he speaking if not the FARL lawyer? Perhaps he was trying to tell me to remain well-disposed towards Arabs in general, but not necessarily towards the FARL in particular.

Obviously, the Service was informed of these contacts, as they were of the visas granted Oriach and the West German militant. After the September bombings, 'they' sent me back to test the atmosphere at the Syrian consulate, but without giving me any precise instructions. Once there, I laid my cards on the table. 'I think the FARL is doing a disservice to the Arab cause,' I said. The diplomat nodded, then dragged me into another room where two people were waiting. Locking the door, he said, 'Now I'm taking you hostage.' He quickly introduced us, then began to talk, deploring the situation in which France found itself, calling the bombings 'abominable, and particularly cowardly'. I raised the stakes, saying that I was considering giving up defending the FARL, but that I still respected the Arab cause, and was prepared to work for it. The idea apparently delighted them . . . and within the next five minutes he asked me to join the Syrian intelligence service! 'Our country has its own, particular, national goals,' he said, 'and we should like you to help us realize them.' I dug in my heels at that, saying that I hadn't even heard his proposition, which I considered an insult both to my position as a lawyer and to me, personally, as a French citizen. Mostly, I think they hoped to use me to obtain additional information about the FARL, or, perhaps, to 'terminate' them without admitting it openly, the members of the group still remaining, officially, their progressivist and revolutionary brothers.

L.G. That was a lot to expect of you: asking you to assume another, and certainly not the easiest, identity. But everything you have said is an indictment of Syria's role in the affair: the quasi-official invitation to Oriach upon his release, the visa granted the member of the Red Army Faction wanted by the police, the attempt to 'turn' a lawyer for the intelligence services. The press has written much about the theory that the FARL, like other revolutionary movements in Europe, may be remote-controlled, or at least supported, by such intelligence services.

J.P.M. That remains in the area of unverifiable conjecture. I favour rather the reverse theory: that Syria, a determinedly progressivist nation, acts as a country of asylum for those militants who are often operating independently. I have no evidence to the contrary.

Many journalists suggest that perhaps in this area Damascus is acting as a front for Soviet influence. The 'Great Satan' theory has always disturbed me, whether it is used by Teheran against Washington, or by the Reaganites against Moscow. I think matters are more complicated than that. Nevertheless, it is true that I was troubled by the extent of the co-operation the FARL claimed it could obtain in any country behind the Iron Curtain. But here, too, I am careful not to generalize. In December 1984, in the face of Syria's refusal to grant me an immediate visa, Abdallah suggested I go to Vienna where I would be contacted and provided with 'authentic' forged Lebanese papers. It is up to those persons who persist in retaining a generalized and systematic view of international terrorism to denounce the presence of Moscow's shadow in every attempt to destabilize the democracies.

|14| THE AGENT

Jean-Paul Mazurier knows that the life of the 'Black Agent' is very different from the glamourized fictions of the spy story. He describes his often ambivalent feelings about his role, its effect on his personal and professional life, and the day-to-day realities of working for the DGSE.

Jean-Paul Mazurier At the beginning my solitude, my powerlessness, had caused me to seek out the authorities. No sooner did the Service contact me, than I was thrown headlong into a life that, I soon realized, I would have to find out about one day at a time.

Laurent Gally Could you have made a different choice?

J.P.M. No. I've thought it over many, many times and don't see how I could have done otherwise. Of course I could have become a police informer but that horrified me, and still does since I consider saying 'I've heard, but of course no one can say you got this from me' as a weak and passive role. I consider it, up to a point, similar to the status of the Service's 'honourable correspondent', although I don't think it's very honourable to inform on a man, or a group, and then wash your hands of the matter and pretend to be holier-than-thou.

But I could have done it, and it would have been easier than what I was trying to do. I could have informed the Service, or the police, at my own pace and not told them everything. And I would not have had to take orders, or undertake exhausting journeys, or have been poisoned. I would not have endangered myself on what, for the average citizen seated in front of his television set, weeping and wailing at the sight of terrorist attacks, is the other side of the world. Or subjected myself to missions which, seen from outside, must have looked like the Keystone Cops, but which I lived through with a belly knotted in fear, furious that I didn't know how to do more, incapable of being like the always-victorious James Bond, or even John Le Carré's little worker-ants, who, in the public's eyes, are the only acceptable sort of spies.

I'm not saying the role of 'black agent' that they offered me, and I accepted, was more honourable. It was a true commitment to the prevention of terrorism and, little by little, became total. I was not against all 'revolutionaries' ' ideas, Pierre Carette's, for example, or the intellectual bases of Abdallah or Joséphine Abdo's position. But I could not bear that their actions should turn against innocent people when I was there, with the secrets I knew, able to influence events, if only a little.

L.G. The choices you made appear incompatible with legal ethics, which demand you defend your clients' interests without taking into account any extraneous issues.

J.P.M. I'm not so sure of that. As a lawyer I defended my clients tooth and nail, whether it was Georges, during his appearance before the examining magistrate (and I was left in no doubt about the judge's disdain for me), or Abdo and Mansuri. I assure you, their acquittal at the Rome trial was not preordained. My Italian colleagues, more comfortable than I in clothing themselves in the majesty of the Law, had not ferreted through the dossier to discover the forged document. And even with that document in their hands, they still preferred an unassertive defence so as not to antagonize the judges, and were content to plead extenuating circumstances. When I wept for joy in Abdo's arms, it was not simply because the young woman's sincerity had moved me, but because I was exhausted, and glad that my fight had not been in vain. I believe I could have swallowed any insult the Service handed me if it would have put an end to the terrorist attacks which were causing so much Parisian blood to be shed.

I'll go even further. Doing my work well was not merely a matter of soothing my conscience, or polishing my left-wing image. It was to show Abdallah and his comrades, perhaps more subtly, that democracies are neither fascist nor imperialist and that, beyond their often confused world-wide diplomatic interests, they care deeply about the Law, and respect the defence, and the rules of adversary procedure. The longer the Law remained unaffected by terrorism, the less justification there was to use violence against our country. Those thoughts sustained me in my determination to deter any acts of terrorism.

L.G. Did the Service ever attempt to oppose you in your determination to fulfil your task as a lawyer?

J.P.M. No. And if they had, I would not have hesitated to disobey their orders. But the *Piscine* is not Manichaean: the Service worked slowly to bring me around to its views, and never once told me that what I was doing, or thinking, was prohibited. On the contrary, my legal success, in Rome for example, suited the *Piscine*, for it brought the FARL to trust me again. And intelligence followed. There was never any thought of casting doubt on my credibility as a defence lawyer. 'They' told me that the Service had sent an observer to the Rome trial, but he did not contact me.

In order to make sure of me, the Service, from the start, set about influencing me. I had met 'Damien', and we did not get along so he was replaced, since the important thing was to gain my trust. The DGSE had become involved with me at very short notice. Up until that moment they had not been on Abdallah's trail and had no photographs, nor description, of him, nor had they tracked down any members of the group. The Service had no choice.

Why did they trust me when I might have been an active FARL sympathizer attempting to penetrate the *Piscine*? Their first guarantee was the opinion of the examining magistrate I had contacted initially. Then there was my approach, no matter how clumsily, to the Security Ministry. Finally, there was my protected status as a lawyer. After all, I could have said nothing, but merely defended Georges to the bitter end. I'm certain that it is a very rare colleague who would spontaneously have taken the position I did. The Service had a choice. If I was lying (as the abortive operations might have made them believe for a while) the *Piscine* would know it very quickly: for example, by decoding Georges' messages, or by failing to track down and identify Jacqueline Esber, or by being unable to stop the suicide truck-bomb in Rome, and so on. And I myself would have 'broken', would have lost myself in the tangle of reports, trips, meetings. I know I was under close surveillance occasionally.

L.G. Did you spot that surveillance? Was that in the regulations?

J.P.M. Easy as it may be to spot classic police surveillance, surveillance by members of the Service was always invisible, often at the price of extraordinary precautions. I remember the tramps around my house, just before a member of the FARL was to visit me before my trip to Belgrade. 'They' would show me pictures of me and my handler sitting in the far corner of some deserted bar. Or 'they' would ask me if what I had eaten with a friend, in a student restaurant, was good. 'They' did everything they could to show me that the surveillance could be both invisible and permanent. But it seems to me that the general rule is slightly different: each agent is, in turn, the object of extremely close surveillance for two or three days, after which he must make a report of all his activities. Each time he forgets an item, or tells even the most harmless lie, he is challenged. That way, everyone becomes used to telling the absolute truth for fear of being caught lying, like a clumsy child, and having to suffer the consequences.

L.G. Does the Service have constant spy scares? What 'punishments' may the Service use to impose discipline?

J.P.M. Since espionage and counter-espionage are the very life blood of the Service, it is obvious that spy scares are built into the system. 'They' spend as much time suspecting their own people as they do their enemies. After meeting certain new contacts I was expected to write evaluation reports. Did they evoke a positive response? Was their physical appearance satisfactory? Were they frank? And so on. I also had to write a report if there was something wrong in the way I was handled by the telephone operators covering the 'secure' numbers when I called from outside France, for example. In a more general way that habit of spying permeated my entire life. I could not dine out, or go to a party, without looking for information that might be of interest to the

171

Service, even if it came from my best friend.

As for maintaining discipline, it is ensured through an almost military scale of punishments: reduction in, or suspension of, one's pay for varying lengths of time; being suspended from the Service, and so on. There are also certain sanctions taken if a mission fails. I have already described my trip to Syria. On my return I was not only suspended for a while, but 'they' told me: 'You're becoming dangerous. You'd better think about your future.'

Although the words were not explicit, the threat was there. And at a time when I had almost totally dropped my normal clientele in favour of the Service, I was suddenly the target of an avalanche of complaints by former clients. I was appearing before the bar disciplinary committee almost daily, accused of having handled cases badly, of having ignored certain legal motions in a particular proceeding, of charging exorbitant fees. Everything that my colleagues normally would have dismissed with a wave of the hand now seemed to be held against me. I defended myself vigorously, but as time passed I began to wonder if perhaps the *Piscine* was not trying to teach me another lesson. 'They' could sink me. 'They' could also help me keep my head above water.

L.G. Did you make any friends among your contacts?

J.P.M. Of the fifteen members of the Service whom I met, some of them only once, as at the meeting attended by a silent 'Monsieur Jean', the staff psychologist, I only had a real relationship with my official handler, 'Antoine'. We met essentially for work reasons, but we also dined together for the sheer pleasure of each other's company, and to talk. I believe he felt true friendship for me and, in any case, I felt it for him. We would spend hours together, eating and drinking, without ever mentioning the Abdallah affair. 'Antoine' told me he envied me, being a professional man. 'If I had what you have,' he often said, 'I'd really know how to make something out of it.' I admired him for his self-assurance, his calmness, his deftness, and even for being in perfect physical condition. That military man reassured me, acting as a sort of 'nanny' and mothering me whenever I became anxious. I know that he defended me several times to my superiors, trying to minimize what he called my 'natural tendency to disobedience'.

He often said that it wasn't easy, keeping me at arm's length.

Higher up in the organization, I met the man who was my actual boss, a colonel in the *Piscine*'s 'Action' section. Our relations were extremely cordial, but the way he spoke softly when giving me my orders was more effective than any outright command could have been. I only saw him a half-dozen times, but if he did come to me for some of my reports it was only after taking elaborate precautions. He was always accompanied by his 'baggage-handler', an armed bodyguard, in Service parlance. 'Antoine' was never without his Beretta, which he carried, classically, in an underarm holster, or in a satchel.

L.G. Were you given any special training, particularly in security measures?

J.P.M. Yes and no. I wasn't taught how to handle a weapon, for example, and 'they' never gave me a pistol for occasions when I might have to defend myself. I also received no training in how to fight off an attacker. My role was so exceptional, and so narrowly defined, that I believe the Service was bent on confining me to my daily schedule and tasks as a lawyer, where I would be most useful to them as a 'black agent'. As for security measures, 'they' only taught me the general rules: try to be aware of being followed and if you are, do not try to shake off the person following you but report it to the Service; try to spot any suspicious cars that may be following you and get the licence-plate number (the Service has a licence-plate file and can quickly tell if the car is 'ours' or not). And there were other rules that applied to all agents but which I had to learn as time went on. And, of course, before each mission (by which the Service also meant my legal work, when I went to visit my clients in jail) I had to sign a declaration on my honour, promising that if I were caught or arrested I would never reveal my ties to the Service, or the object of my mission.

L.G. Is it possible for an agent to have a private life?

J.P.M. I suppose it is, if he's married, faithful, has children and a normal home life. But the Service does not tolerate even the smallest indiscretion. At the very beginning they asked for photographs and a brief *curriculum vitae* not only of my girlfriend, but of my closest acquaintances. I was forbidden to meet journalists, who the Service called 'muck-rakers'. Any one of these things could set off an investigation, or cause someone to be followed, to prevent an agent falling into a trap because of his private life. The Service even investigates chance encounters. I was indiscreet, during one of my trips to Italy. The young lady was pretty, and I had succumbed to her charms for a night or two. I was forced to confess, which set off an investigation to see if the girl was actually who she said she was. All this is exhausting. You have to lie to people to keep your real work secret and you end up feeling as if you're lying all the time, never being able to open up to people, which is the very basis of love and friendship. The hardest part is not saying anything to the woman you love, and with whom you are living.

L.G. Were your fiancée, and later, your girlfriends aware of anything? Did they ask questions?

J.P.M. Of course. I had to hide whenever I wanted to make or receive certain telephone calls. When I left on a mission I had to say that I was tired and was going to take a few days' holiday by myself, without leaving an address where I could be reached. All that wouldn't necessarily lead someone to think of espionage, but within a couple it does tend to make her question one's faithfulness. And it's the same whether you say something or don't: often it is better to say nothing than to lie. According to my handler, his wife knows only that he works as a civil servant. The Service ordered me not to say anything to my fiancée, but she wasn't born yesterday. Several times she tried to ask me for an explanation, tried to find out who was the mysterious 'Antoine' with whom I was always talking on the telephone . . . I side-stepped her questions, told lies, and slowly we grew further apart and, finally, broke up. You just try explaining that you're going somewhere for a rest and come back from Syria ten days later, exhausted and suffering from the after-effects of poisoning, your spirits low, and needing months of medical care before you're well again!

L.G. Describe your meetings with the Service.

J.P.M. The only constant was that each meeting was surrounded by incredible precautionary measures. Security measures varied, according to whom I was meeting, where we were to meet, etc. At the beginning I met my handler in a restaurant, and we would go for a walk, moving in a zigzag pattern to make sure we were not being followed. We were suspicious of everyone: the FARL, agents of other, foreign intelligence services, even the police. We did not want anyone sticking his nose in our business. I was supposed never to take the Metro to a meeting with my contact without first getting out at a station that had been chosen in advance, letting a train pass and then, if it was safe, taking the following train. Of course there were other agents, whom I did not know, on the platform, making certain nobody was following me as I changed trains.

Later, a car would often wait for me near my office. I would come out exactly at a predetermined time, and walk following a route that had been marked out in advance. There would be a second car covering me, again to spot anyone who might be following.

Most often our meetings took place in bistros, or in hotel rooms rented for the occasion. The hotel rooms were impersonal, my handler had the key, and we would manage to take the same lift but pretend not to know each other. The sort of meeting usually took place a day or two before I was to leave on a mission, and the conversation could go on for hours. The room cost three or four hundred francs, and since one never heard any noise I assumed the Service had rented the adjacent rooms as well.

I also had meetings on park benches, in city squares, in the open. Nothing was ever discussed at those meetings; I would merely hand over my reports. I remember once waiting a full day in the snow, stoic but freezing, in the garden of a maternity clinic. Not one nurse came out to inquire about the state of my mental health.

L.G. Were your reports oral, or written?

J.P.M. During the first six months I made only oral reports. I would read Abdallah's messages over the phone, and make an extremely detailed synopsis of our conversations in the visitors' room. Several months later 'they' demanded that I begin making written reports, the reason officially being that there might be distortions between what I said and the information or organization finally received. I cannot exclude the possibility that 'they' wanted to have at their disposal as many handwritten documents as possible so as to have a means of pressuring me if the need arose. Before that, there had been no proof of my activities for the *Piscine*. Now the situation had changed, but to their profit only. For my part, I still had no proof, which is why I recorded certain telephone calls from the Service to my office, just in case. Those recordings are in a safe place, to make doubly certain, and I have left precise instructions. I remember one of the rules 'Christian' taught me: 'Keep an ace up your sleeve . . .'

L.G. Do you think the *Piscine* will take retaliatory measures against you when this book is published?

J.P.M. I'm not a prophet, but it's obvious I'm completely breaking the rules. But I can state positively that I am in no way working against the image, or security, of the Service. On the contrary, I believe that although we may criticize the DGSE and consider it ineffective, notably against Middle-Eastern terrorism, my story tends to prove the opposite, even though we were unable to thwart in advance the heaviest wave of terrorism.

Abdallah, himself, had praise for the DGSE. The very people he had called 'little boys' at the beginning had, little by little, become dangerous adversaries whom he compared to Mossad. This, coming from him, is really something when you realize how effective the Israelis are in fighting Middle-Eastern terrorism.

L.G. Does an agent leave the Service without regrets?

J.P.M. In theory, it is not you who leaves the Service; it is the Service that leaves you. But I don't know how this maxim, customary amongst *Piscine* agents, can be unconditional. I do not confuse my own work, and any information I may have uncovered, with a military career spent in intelligence. I was acting out of humanitarian concerns, because of my horror of terrorism. Now I believe the situation has stabilized somewhat, not so much through the Service's efforts as due to the general political and diplomatic situation. This is beyond a mere mortal like me, but I'm happy about it, and I hope it will last. This also undercuts any pretentions I may have. There are numerous means of action, and though the information I provided was certainly useful, it was perhaps not decisive. More traditional means of intelligence-gathering are in operation, the Abdallah affair has made its way through the court system, and every French citizen is free to measure its extent, and complexity.

As for the life of a spy, I had known nothing about it before becoming one and cannot tell if I experienced any more than its usual constraints: impossible hours, the demand that one be available at all times, the feeling of heading into danger, the fear, and so on. Those two years of total commitment drained me. Being tied to the Abdallah case, and to the day-to-day prison life of militant revolutionaries with whom I had nothing in common, impoverished every area of my life. However, and this may seem curious, the very idea of leaving the Service has given me a sort of nostalgia for it. Hiding the spy behind the lawyer, the lawyer behind the spy, and trying at the same time to live a normal private life had transformed my existence into a permanent lie. The only truthful time, sometimes shockingly so, was during my conversations with my handler, and my superiors.

L.G. Did you approve of all their ideas, all their methods?

J.P.M. The Service told me I was the one who had set the Abdallah machine in motion. But I had only begun it; they never told me what else was set in motion after that. I have no illusions. The DGSE is part of the Ministry of Defence, and half the people who work there are professional soldiers who consider themselves to be at war around the clock, especially against terrorism. They use all the methods of war: those infamous 'terminations' are inevitably within the compass of the operations or 'Action' section. 'They' didn't tell me this. I heard it from Abdallah.

'Because of your carelessness, comrades have been killed,' he said, fatalistically and with apparent detachment, in August 1985 after the FARL internal investigation. 'It isn't serious, but you must be more alert from now on.' I shuddered, and his next words twisted the knife in the wound. 'You know, a hundred comrades may fall, but you, you are irreplaceable.'

I have no illusions about the methods that are used (though the argument that one must get one's hands dirty in order to accomplish anything is still open to question) nor about the opinions held by some Service agents. They're quite straightforward: all revolutionaries are terrorists and aren't worth the rope needed to hang them. The words used when talking about them seldom varied: bastards, swine, murderers. Abdallah was never that categorical. Once, talking about the Greenpeace affair, he expressed admiration at the scope of the operation the DGSE had organized half-way around the world. When I reported his favourable opinion to my handler, he turned pensive: 'Damn; to think the only congratulations we've had come from terrorists . . .'

I systematically avoided discussing politics, or introducing the notion of relative morality into our conversations. In my written reports I attempted to put my clients' thoughts and positions into perspective. I'm not saying the entire Service is right wing; far from it. A number of my contacts assured me that they 'voted left'.

L.G. The ideas and methods used by security agencies are the same everywhere.

J.P.M. Although their objectives may be the same (to protect their own vital interests, through the use of force if necessary) the tactics used vary considerably. According to Georges, Mossad is the only agency to systematically destroy all means of communication within a network, in order to totally disorganize it. And since the militants, themselves, are the means, there is probably a constant threat of death. Georges says that other Western intelligence agencies, like the DGSE, allow the small-fry to act, and follow them as far up the ladder as possible towards the top, then pull everyone in, including the leaders.

In the case of the FARL, Georges seemed to be its leader. But once he was in prison, the *Piscine* wanted to learn who might replace him on the ground, if that replacement would be temporary or permanent, and, above all, if someone else was pulling the strings. That was for the long term. Of course in the short term, they wanted to deter any terrorist attacks that might be committed by the rank and file.

There is another problem with terrorist organizations. All intelligence agencies are aware that new generations of militants are constantly being trained for action, like a phoenix rising from its own ashes. In this connection, Georges wanted to send me to

Lebanon in December 1984. 'Go to Shtaura,' he said. 'Go to the pastry shop on the main square. See the owner, and ask him to introduce you to Georges. You'll meet someone who looks like me, even to the beard . . .' The Service had established that the torch probably had been passed on to Maurice Ibrahim Abdallah, Georges' brother, somewhat in the same manner that the leader of the Armenian ASALA adopts the symbolic name Agop Agopian, no matter what his real identity.

|15| JEAN-PAUL

Jean-Paul Mazurier's character and motives have attracted much comment throughout his association with the Abdallah case. What is he really like? And what are the influences which have created the complex individual revealed in these pages? He talks frankly about his family background, his personal life, his career as a lawyer, and the implications of his current situation.

Jean-Paul Mazurier Now, at the age of thirty-two, I sometimes wonder if my life isn't all behind me. The two years I spent working for the *Piscine* so marked me, and rendered my future so uncertain, that this book constitutes a turning point in my existence. Soon now I shall no longer be a lawyer, no longer be a member of the Service. The conclusion of the Abdallah affair, although not yet official, will be bitter for me.

Laurent Gally Is your decision to resign from the bar irrevocable?

J.P.M. I am going public about belonging to the Service and, since I prefer to make the first move, have already sent in my letter of resignation from the bar. Of course there are a few cases I regret having to abandon, particularly the one of a hired killer towards whom I felt a sort of instant sympathy, his life having been so heavily marked by bad luck, and mental and economic misery. I would have liked to see that case through to the end, as well as several others, but I no longer have the choice of waiting. I will also miss no longer pleading cases at the Assizes, the one arena where a lawyer may play out his role to its fullest, perhaps even more so than in the examining magistrates' offices.

L.G. Was being a lawyer a vocation for you?

J.P.M. Not at all, for after taking my baccalaureat in science at the age of seventeen, I began the study of medicine. But that, too, was not by vocation. Like so many other parents, mine hoped their son would become a professional man, which to them implied independence, money and respect. I spent three years trying to finish one year of medical school, but I wasn't cut out for it. Successful as I was in the scientific, technical, and academic parts of the final examinations, I was incapable of sitting for the second, decisive portion. I came down with glandular fever and, the next year, herpetic tonsilitis. I was psychosomatically acting out my mental block.

I switched to law, but I could have done it either way: law first, then medicine. I had no passion for education, even though I was a good student. I dreamed only of motor racing.

I took a course in racing driving, which fascinated me, driving what they call Renault Formula cars. I reached the finals but was beaten by Charles Cevert, brother of the well-known Formula 1 driver who had just been killed at Watkins Glen, in the United States. Racing filled me with unfamiliar, exciting sensations: a taste for taking risks, overcoming fears; the finesse and intellectual effort needed to analyze the track; concentration, a sense of competition. Looking back now, I am convinced it is the only thing I ever truly liked: putting my life and my fate on the line, testing myself against the road, depending on nothing but an engine and a chassis, and not on people or political ideology, as I do now. Like so many other adolescents I dreamed of glory, of money, of having women at my feet, which in young people's minds is how Formula 1 drivers live, racing against death and then relaxing in luxury.

L.G. As a young man, were you attracted to death?

J.P.M. No, not as such. On the contrary, I was physically disgusted by it. When I was a medical student I watched autopsies, and saw the dissected bodies of old people and was not bothered by it. Then one day, our professor began sawing open the skull of a young man who resembled me. From that moment on I had no further interest in my studies. From a very young age, and this probably stems from my relationship with my parents, and with life in general, I went in for all kinds of high-risk, almost suicidal, activities, as if I had to gamble with my life in order to be able to accept it. Motor racing first, then a passion for motorcycles, alcohol and other drugs and, finally, joining the Service. I did not go into it with an image of James Bond in my mind; far from it. For me it was a way of racing full speed ahead, of living my life on the edge, on a high-wire, knowing that it would snap by itself, with no help from me.

L.G. How did all this lead you back to the law?

J.P.M. Life is not linear, and I was not behaving suicidally all the time. After failing my medical studies I had to find something to take their place. Law was a last resort, and the classes gave me time to live another sort of life, to wander. Having been forced to repeat my fourth year, I thought I might try for a CAPA, a Certificate of Aptitude for the Legal Profession. Many young people will recognize themselves in the story of my academic career. It took me two years to earn my CAPA, and I spent a total of five years studying law.

I immediately fell in love with my work as a lawyer. I had found a mentor, an experienced lawyer who took me on as a trainee in his firm, where I was to learn the profession hands-on. By the end of the year I had enough clients to open my own law practice. During that period I worked long hours, and was lucky. Not that I was earning much money. When I began my law practice I was twenty-six years old, and had seen so much human misery, so many people dependent on procedures which were Greek to them, that the responsibility seemed overwhelming. When it reads about cases in the newspapers, the public doesn't see much difference between a three-year, or a ten-year sentence; but for the lawyer watching his client going under, it's a nightmare. With every case that ended in an unfavourable decision, I would lose my sleep and my appetite. I had pains in my chest and a stomach ulcer that, after treatment, turned into gastritis. I was taking the weight of the world on my shoulders. Entering the profession, we have the feeling that Justice is a bride whose train we must bear; it is only later we come to realize we must rape her, if we are to accomplish anything.

L.G. Is that more or less a commitment?

J.P.M. I became a lawyer with no thought of social advancement, but the profession captured first my heart and then my mind. It's impossible to think of the world as being perfect when you see so much misery revealed in your office.

I am tenacious to the point of being unbearable to others, which led to my left-wing reputation at the Palais de Justice. But above all I am a man who does his homework, who tries to find the flaws, the holes, the misinterpretations in the prosecution's case. Through lack of talent, or shyness, I don't speak well in public, except when I am pleading a case with my heart and guts; at such times I've been known to make jurors weep.

L.G. Since you have a true feeling for the legal profession, how did you manage to carry out both your jobs at the same time?

J.P.M. I never succeeded in reconciling the two, which placed me in the painful, and perhaps to others incomprehensible, position of acting as both lawyer and spy. I had not joined the Service to arrest terrorists, but simply to prevent blind violence against innocent people. It was not altruism. As a spoiled only child, I had hated violence since I was very young.

These feelings intensified after I was the victim of a mugging, in England. I was fifteen at the time and, like many French school-children, had gone there to improve my English. One evening around nine o'clock, on my way home to my host family in a London suburb, I was attacked by a gang of skinheads. According to witnesses, since it happened too fast for me to see them, there were approximately a dozen skinheads of about my own age. They hit me from behind with an iron bar. As I lay huddled on the ground I heard them say, 'Kill him, kill him.'

I don't know who scared them off, but I was taken to a hospital and operated on for a smashed nose and a skull fracture between my eyes, not to mention other facial injuries, and bruises. I underwent a total of four operations. My first reaction, while they were beating me, was: 'If I get out of this, I'll take a machine-gun and shoot them all down, if I can find them again.' Once my convalescence was over, and I had had time to calm down, I realized that, given the same childhood, I might have been part of that gang beating up a Frenchman or, living in France, beating up Arabs without really knowing why I was doing it. They were not much older than I, and probably from a poorer background. They were underprivileged, even though they *were* bastards. I never brought charges against them, thinking that I was giving them a chance to lead a 'normal' life.

I'm not trying to make myself out to be better than I am. After that mugging I felt an instinctive hatred for the whole human race. The mugging changed many things for me, my brush with death perhaps making me realize I actually existed. The result was that I became detached and philosophical, if not suicidal, telling myself: 'After all, it's only me who is dying.' That was also what flashed through my mind when I had my motorcycle accident, early in 1984.

L.G. Might your suicidal behaviour be linked to the mugging? Did you have psychiatric treatment in order to try to deal with the trauma?

J.P.M. I did not see a psychologist after the mugging and only entered psychoanalysis some twelve years later. In the course of my therapy I mentioned that night in London, but in positive terms. I consider it an educational experience that taught me about violence as an outlet, about types of reactions, about the social bases of racism, and so on. I had been the victim of a lynch mob; I tried to understand why.

Psychoanalysis itself did not do much for me, but that was my own fault. I started early in 1982, before meeting Abdallah. My psychiatrist's office was outside Paris and the appointments, each of which, including travelling time, took up almost half a day, were incompatible with my work schedule. I was not feeling particularly at odds with myself, but I had gone into the study of medicine with the idea of becoming an analyst, and an analysis was necessary before I could move on to the next step, self-analysis. My analyst soon gave me a salutary lesson. Knowing I wanted to exercise his profession, he sent me one of his patients who was suffering from a persecution complex and wanted a lawyer to protect her interests, which she believed were being threatened. Dealing with this woman, who refused to open her mouth during our hour-long meetings, I came to understand the profession was far more difficult than I had believed and, through inertia, gradually let the idea drop.

Recently, for other reasons, I again started analysis, or rather psychotherapy. Deeply disturbed by my activities and unable to confide in anyone, I went to see a psychiatrist with the almost perverse notion of paying a professional to listen to me complain and rage against my isolation, but without telling him I was a spy. The couch on which I lie down twice a week for forty-five minutes, during which I am free to talk or to say nothing, is my own private Switzerland: a protected, neutral territory where only monetary relations rule.

L.G. Is the fact you have now chosen to go public an attempt at a psychoanalytic explanation of your actions, an attempt at justification?

J.P.M. I wanted to explain what happened to me. I don't care at all what my readers may think, or what opinion my colleagues may have of me. I have reached a point of saturation, exasperation, and weariness. Looking back, I have the feeling of having reached a point of no return.

L.G. What made you an outsider?

J.P.M. That's hard to say. The day I was sworn in at the bar, I met a girl. It was love at first sight, and we became engaged. We planned to marry a year later, but we were from very different social classes. Daughter of a well-known solicitor, she introduced me into a family whose way of life was nothing like my own. Since I had to work all the time in order to provide her with those things to which her father had accustomed her, we had very little time together. Our times apart grew longer, and instead of preparing myself to take over from her father, as it was more or less understood I would do, it was our relationship that broke down first. So I said goodbye to a bourgeois existence, which I wasn't made for anyway. But I deny I have a vocation for living life on the edge. From the very start my career simply took off, my reputation was growing, and I had no financial problems.

In 1982, when 'Alex' first came to see me, I was merely one lawyer among hundreds of others with a rising career. But circumstances caused our paths to cross and I decided to accept the propositions the Service made me, for reasons I believe I have repeated here far too often. I performed certain acts, I have no particular feelings about that. I tried to obey orders, doing what I considered to be my duty.

What struck me, during my first meeting with the *Piscine* colonel who was my superior, was his saying: 'Now you are one of us, Jean-Paul. You must realize that, like us, you are now and will remain on the fringes of society.' Coming from a superior officer, those words seemed incongruous and I didn't see the need for them. Since then, alas, I have understood.

L.G. Do you feel alone, more alone than before you joined the Service.

J.P.M. Yes, and this book won't help. As a teenager I dreamed of being Fangio, of being admired by the crowd for my lonely courage. Now I have learned to live with that isolation: it weighs heavily on me since I have never been able to confide in anyone. At the same time, it always seemed to me that isolation was an essential condition for my own safety, almost a means of survival.

The worst part is not the isolation but the effects it produces. For I am a lone wolf who does not like being alone. I almost became an alcoholic, was tempted to take drugs, I would knock myself out with sleeping pills simply because, at times, I needed to be numb, to forget my anxieties and my anguish.

L.G. Do you think you were born to be a spy? Didn't the Service err regarding the nature and the extent of your motives?

J.P.M. In any case, they hardly had a choice. I was offering them an unexpected lead. I was sincere, I played the game. But the thought of joining up for life . . . I'm rather cold, by nature, master of my emotions and feelings. I never let my thoughts show. Certainly I was not an ideal agent, although each one has his own story, and any attempt at analysis would open up a can of worms, but I was indispensable for this job. My personal ideas did not necessarily coincide with those of my superiors. My role, which I had intended strictly as a preventive one in the struggle against terrorism, has no more meaning today.

I have no desire to spy on the thoughts and actions of the people around me. I no longer want to lie or be obliged to live in the shadows, even if it means starting my life all over again. My motives remain the same. I openly declare my opposition to terrorism, without finding fault with the Service's methods. Was I cowardly, or courageous? Those words have no meaning for me. I did what I could, with the means at my disposal. When you find yourself at a crossroads one day and you have a chance – or you think you do – to put an end to a monstrosity, you don't hesitate, you don't even stop to think.

L.G. How will your friends react to this book?

J.P.M. Their reactions will vary according to the relationship I have with them. The most difficult part will be my parents' reaction. They don't really know me. They cling to an idea they have of me. Nevertheless I worry about their opinion, even though I feel this book doesn't reflect the whole me. In this book I have described myself rather than revealed myself.

Like so many only sons, I have a fairly unhealthy relationship with my parents. My mother, a former schoolteacher, surrounded me with suffocating love and tenderness. She wanted me to enter a profession, while at the same time assuring me I would never amount to anything. She is a very curious person, very suspicious, and whenever I am at her house listens in on my telephone conversations, so that the Service began to tease me about her.

'France has three intelligence agencies,' 'Antoine' would joke, 'the DST, the DGSE, and your mother. And she's the most dangerous.'

The fact is that over the last two years, no matter what she might have thought or guessed, she kept quiet, and I am grateful to her. My father, too, can barely understand what I have done. He has had an extremely difficult life, working from the time he was thirteen then, before the Second World War, becoming a professional soccer player with the Paris Racing Club team. What followed was scarcely better: military service in 1937, the general mobilization, the war, prison camps, and three unfruitful escape attempts. When I was young he often said, speaking of the intelligence services: 'And to think they couldn't even manage to warn us in 1940.' His opinion was reconfirmed during the Greenpeace affair, which he considered to be an act of state-sponsored terrorism.

Some of my few remaining friends may take this book the wrong way, or be offended by it. In these last few years I have so often taken refuge behind a mask that my attitude or, rather, my failure to confide in them, can only be wounding. Orson Welles claimed that all men unconsciously pursue one of three myths: Faust, Don Juan, or Don Quixote. My friends know my inconstancy, yet who can resist being Don Juan? My acquaintances think of me as the eternal adolescent: I don't look my age and, very young, refused to grow up. Abdallah could have called me 'a lion cub', like Mansuri. I, too, have little facial hair. But the Faust myth is more dangerous in other ways, even if the *Piscine* is not the Devil.

There remains the third myth which perhaps applies to my life over the last two years. Was I not playing Don Quixote, jousting with windmills? I have no doubts about the validity of my aims, the need to deter terrorism, but when all is said and done, I no longer know if I accomplished anything.

I do not know what tomorrow will bring. I was not at the defence table when Abdallah appeared before the Paris Assize Court, which was specially composed of seven judges. I did not attend the trial as I had no wish to see Georges again nor to hear that type of discourse again. Soon, I shall no longer be a lawyer, nor an agent. I may be dead, but I shall be Jean-Paul.

L.G. After this book, how can you still support Abdallah?

J.P.M. The question has become theoretical since it is no longer permissible for me to do so. In any case, people will not understand which mask was speaking, the lawyer or the 'black agent', and I have decided to rid myself of both of them. Not to mention that some would have wanted to find a few more reasons for indicting Georges in this tale, and that he will no longer have anything to do with me.

L.G. Are you using this book to inform the Service of your resignation?

J.P.M. Of course, since there is no other way to do it. The

Piscine has tried to 'reactivate' me. At the beginning of December 'they' again asked me to go into the field, in Damascus. I didn't know what to say. Orders are meant to be obeyed, not discussed. But I'm afraid, I'm tired, I want to put an end to it. I'm no longer motivated, I no longer believe in the effectiveness of what I do.

L.G. Are you afraid of reprisals?

J.P.M. Yes. This book isn't meant as a defiant gesture, but the number of people who will blame me for it will be legion, powerful, and armed. I thought of going somewhere, anywhere, a long way away. I then gave up this illusory attempt to keep myself out of harm's way. I want to take responsibility for my position, to tell my version of the events, to explain how, and at what cost – personal cost, in my case – certain people are struggling to protect the great mass of innocent people. I hope the masks that have been removed here will no longer cling to me, will no longer invade my thoughts. I want to start my life again, as myself.

Perhaps there will be reprisals. I have considered them, from the 'hit-and-run' accident to the possibility of a bullet in the head from some enraged 'revolutionary' meting out 'proletarian justice', as they call it. Death is one of the paths I may take. I no longer have a choice, so I've developed a sort of forced serenity, an obligatory calm. But should this turn out to be the case, by my death the prospective killer – no matter what his organization – will have proved me right. If this book disturbs people to the point of their exacting vengeance by assassinating me, it will be because the truth I have tried to tell seems unbearable . . . perhaps because of its very banality.

L.G. In any case, the struggle against terrorism, as well as revolutionary militancy, will go on.

J.P.M. Yes. I'm simply removing myself from the game, voluntarily. Four years ago I found myself at a crossroads, and refused to commit myself. Then, feeling guilty for my behaviour, I wholeheartedly attempted to deter any new outbreaks of terrorism for two years. Reality swept my hopes away, as the Service's actions (no matter how effective they might have been at the time) became influenced by political and diplomatic considerations. I want no more to do with that chessboard. I am going back to being a private citizen, like any other. Have I been cowardly, or courageous? Then, or now? These words mean nothing to me. Circumstances forced me to commit certain acts. I have no particular feelings about them.

For me, the war is over.

Paris, 17 September 1986
to January 1987

EPILOGUE

Jean-Paul Mazurier is still alive, but he is no longer a lawyer. The day after this book was published he voluntarily resigned from the Paris bar, in the face of the backlash provoked by his actions. For it is not easy to step out of one's allotted role, and society – French society, at least – does not appreciate the confusion it causes. Although this does not apply to the whole of society: far from it. After the appearance of this book Jean-Paul Mazurier received hundreds of letters, none of them anonymous. Every one of them, as I can testify, contained messages of congratulations, of sympathy, of encouragement to take up his life again.

His brother lawyers, however, did not pass the same judgement. They finally struck him off the register of the Paris bar, the supreme sanction for a lawyer since it means a total professional ban. The reason given was that Mazurier had violated the oath of his profession – to defend and only defend his client – but he was not, in the end, censured for having committed a breach of professional confidence.

Beyond that, this book itself almost failed to see the light of day. The French government demanded its partial seizure – and the appendices which appeared in the original document had to be withdrawn – to preserve 'defence secrets'. Without returning to the judicial decision which justified the government's action – for what jurist can define, in practice, 'defence secrets' – it should be established that the seizure was demanded the day after the Paris

Assize Court verdict condemning Georges Ibrahim Abdallah to life imprisonment. Can one see a relationship of cause and effect? The press did not fail to point out that the charges against Abdallah were inexplicably weak and vague, and that the judges had more or less rebelled against the government's wishes in deciding on the longest penalty in French law for Abdallah. The seizure of the book could be seen as 'setting aside' the trial verdict, or at least as leaving a judicial door open, before new and discreet contacts with the 'godparents' of the Lebanese militant. Since then the situation has altered. Feelings have calmed, and the Middle-Eastern powder-keg again centres on Iran and its fundamentalist cohorts.

The fact remains that at no time, whatever the contents of the text or the banned appendices, have the statements and disclosures made in this book been contested. The freedom of the press remains a fact. The authorities knew that this book, written as a moral imperative after the Rue de Rennes bombing in September 1986, was printed a month before Abdallah's trial, but was not put on sale so as not to affect the course of justice. Even so a sheriff's officer, anxious to comply with the court's decisions, got a date wrong and ordered the burning of 18,000 copies in stock containing the disputed appendices.

Has the curtain now come down on the story? Some people will think that the state gives poor recompense to those who serve it. They may also think that Jean-Paul Mazurier suffers alone for a fickle reason of state. It relates to the official dumbness and judicial silence which surrounded the politicians and soldiers responsible for the 'Greenpeace' affair, in which even those who took part in the commando raid on the *Rainbow Warrior* were not charged with attempted homicide or causing destruction with explosives.

Today only a trace remains of the remarkable adventure of this young lawyer: a double, triple character, torn apart by his conscience, his fascination with death and his hatred of violence. For years, Jean-Paul Mazurier wandered down endless corridors lined with distorting mirrors. Now he has shattered them all, voluntarily, violently. He has emerged all but destroyed. His life belongs to himself from now on.

Laurent Gally

Appendix: FARL Activities and Associated Events 1981-7

Paris, 12 November 1981:
Attempted assassination of Christian Adison Chapman, second-highest ranking diplomat at the American Embassy, Paris. A full magazine of 7.65-calibre ammunition is emptied at his car, but the diplomat escapes unharmed. In a letter, the FARL claims responsibility for the attack.

Paris, 18 January 1982:
Execution of Lieutenant-Colonel Charles Ray, Military Attaché at the American Embassy, by a 7.65-calibre bullet to the head, Boulevard Emile-Augier, Paris. A letter from the FARL claiming responsibility for the murder referred to President Reagan's policies in El Salvador and Lebanon.

Paris, 31 March 1982:
Machine-gun attack on the building occupied by the Israeli consulate's purchasing office on the Boulevard Malesherbes. The FARL claims responsibility for the attack, by means of leaflets, with the logistical help of Action Directe (according to investigators Action Directe militants sent out the leaflets and may also have been responsible for retrieving the machine-gun used in the attack).

Paris, 3 April 1982:
Yacov Barsimantov, Second Secretary at the Israeli Embassy in France, is murdered outside his Paris house. His son, witness to the murder, chases a young woman who shot his father – the weapon is a 7.65-calibre automatic – as far as the nearest Metro entrance. The son gives the police a description of the murderer – large space between the front teeth, wide hips – which leads the police to nickname Jacqueline Esber 'Bigass'. Responsibility for the murder claimed by the FARL.

Paris, 22 August 1982:
American commercial attaché Roderick Grant's booby-trapped car explodes in the Avenue de la Bourdonnais, killing two Prefecture of Police bomb-disposal experts, Bernard le Dreau and Bernard Mauron, as they are defusing it. The FARL later claims responsibility.

Paris, 17 September 1982:
A car belonging to the Israeli Embassy in Paris, explodes in front of the Lycée Carnot causing numerous injuries among the students; two diplomats are gravely wounded. Leaflets claiming FARL responsibility 'in the name of anti-imperialism' are distributed by persons the police suspect to be militants belonging to Action Directe.

Rome, 15 February 1984:
Assassination of Leamon Hunt, American diplomat and former director of the Multinational Force in the Sinai. Three groups claim responsibility: among them the Italian Red Brigades and FARL.

Paris, 26 March 1984:
The Consul General of the United States in Strasbourg, Robert Onan Homme, is gravely wounded by three 7.65-calibre bullets. FARL claims responsibility for the attack.

Trieste, 6 August 1984:
Arrested on the Ljubljana-Milan-Paris express, Mohammed el-Mansuri is found to be carrying a forged Moroccan passport and seven kilograms of explosives in his suitcase.

Lyons, 24 October 1984:
Arrest of Saadi Abdelkader, an Algerian citizen, by agents of the DST. Abdelkader, whom it will later be learned is actually Georges Ibrahim Abdallah, is also carrying a forged Maltese passport and twenty thousand dollars in cash.

Zurich, 25 November 1984:
Arrest at Zurich Airport of Hani Hussein, a Lebanese national on his way to Rome, carrying two kilograms of explosives.

Rome, end of November 1984:
Arrest of seven Lebanese nationals discovered preparing a suicide truck-bomb attack against the American Embassy.

Beirut, 22 March 1985:
Kidnapping of two French diplomats, Marcel Carton and Marcel Fontaine. Responsibility claimed by Islamic Jihad.

Tripoli, northern Lebanon, 24 March 1985:
Kidnapping of Gilles Sidney Peyroles, director of the French Cultural Centre, by the FARL. Peyroles is released on April 2nd, theoretically in exchange for a promise that France will soon expel Abdallah.

Paris, 8 April 1985:
Police reveal they have discovered a FARL arsenal in an apartment rented by Esber and Abdallah, 18 Rue Lacroix, Paris. A Czechoslovakian-made 7.65-calibre automatic found there is, according to ballistics experts, the weapon used in the Ray and Barsimantov assassinations. Abdallah is indicted for complicity in murder.

Cairo, 7 October 1985:
Hijacking of the Italian cruiseship *Achille Lauro*, by the Palestine Liberation Front, a branch of Yasser Arafat's PLO. Concurrently, opening of the trial, in Rome, of Joséphine Abdo and Mohammed el-Mansuri, who are acquitted.

Paris, 7 December 1985:
Two bomb explosions in the Galeries Lafayette and Printemps department stores leave thirty-five wounded among the crowd of Christmas shoppers. During further bombings in February 1986, responsibility for these attacks will be claimed by the CSPPA, The Committee for Solidarity with Arab and Near-Eastern Political Prisoners, a branch of the FARL, according to investigators. The CSPPA demands the simultaneous release of Georges Ibrahim Abdallah, the pro-Iranian Anis Naccache (leader of a commando group that had attacked the former Iranian Prime Minister, Shapur Bakhtiar), and of the Armenian Warujian Garabejian, sentenced to prison for a terrorist attack at Orly Airport in July 1983.

Paris, 3, 4, 5 February 1986:
Three bombs explode in the Claridge Gallery on the Champs-Elysées, at the Gibert Jeune bookshop on the Boulevard Saint-Michel, and at the FNAC sporting goods store at the Forum des Halles underground shopping mall in central Paris. Nineteen wounded.

TGV (Train à Grande Vitesse), Paris-Lyons, 17 March 1986:
A bomb explodes, leaving ten wounded. The CSPPA claims responsibility for the attack.

Paris, 20 March 1986:
A bomb explodes in the Point-Show Gallery on the Champs-Elysées, at the moment the names of members of the new government, led by Jacques Chirac, are being announced. Responsibility for the bombing, which leaves two dead and twenty-eight wounded, is claimed by the CSPPA, and follows by a few days the confirmation of the guilty verdicts against Abdo and Mansuri in

Trieste. On the same day, a bomb attempt fails in an RER train, Châtelet Station, Paris.

Lyons, 10 July 1986:
Georges Ibrahim Abdallah is sentenced to four years in prison for 'associating with criminals' and the possession of explosives. Following the verdict, the United States government expresses its 'surprise' at the 'light' sentence, and constitutes itself *'partie civile'* in the case being prepared against Abdallah in Paris.

Paris, 4-7 September 1986:
Six terrorist attacks are committed, and responsibility for them claimed by the CSPPA. On the 4th, a failed bomb attack on an RER train at the Gare de Lyon. On the 8th, one dead and eighteen wounded in a bomb explosion at the Hôtel de Ville (Town Hall) post office, Paris. On the 12th, forty-one wounded in the Casino supermarket cafeteria, Quatre-Temps shopping centre, La Défense, on the western edge of Paris. On the 14th, two dead and one wounded at the Pub Renault, Champs-Elysées. On the 15th, one dead and fifty-one wounded after a bomb explodes at the Motor Vehicle Bureau, Prefecture of Police, Paris. On the 17th, seven dead and fifty-one wounded in front of the Tati discount store, Rue de Rennes, Paris, after a bomb is thrown from a passing car. Maurice and Robert Abdallah, brothers of Georges Ibrahim Abdallah, are, in turn, accused by the French police, and hold successive press conferences, in Lebanon, to declare their innocence.

Paris, 23 December 1986:
Gilles Boulouque, the examining magistrate, completes the Abdallah dossier in the Ray, Barsimantov and Homme cases, and delivers them to the prosecutor's office.

Paris, 28 January 1987:
The Public Prosecutor decides to bring the leader of the FARL to trial at the Paris Assizes which, for this occasion, will be composed of seven judges. The trial opens on 23 February 1987.

By order of the Superior Court of Paris, 2 March 1987, the documents comprising the original Appendix were suppressed from this present edition.

(signed)
The Publisher
of the French Edition

FOR THE BEST IN PAPERBACKS, LOOK FOR THE (🐧)

In every corner of the world, on every subject under the sun, Penguin represents quality and variety – the very best in publishing today.

For complete information about books available from Penguin – including Pelicans, Puffins, Peregrines and Penguin Classics – and how to order them, write to us at the appropriate address below. Please note that for copyright reasons the selection of books varies from country to country.

In the United Kingdom: For a complete list of books available from Penguin in the U.K., please write to *Dept E.P., Penguin Books Ltd, Harmondsworth, Middlesex, UB7 0DA*

In the United States: For a complete list of books available from Penguin in the U.S., please write to *Dept BA, Penguin, 299 Murray Hill Parkway, East Rutherford, New Jersey 07073*

In Canada: For a complete list of books available from Penguin in Canada, please write to *Penguin Books Canada Ltd, 2801 John Street, Markham, Ontario L3R 1B4*

In Australia: For a complete list of books available from Penguin in Australia, please write to the *Marketing Department, Penguin Books Australia Ltd, P.O. Box 257, Ringwood, Victoria 3134*

In New Zealand: For a complete list of books available from Penguin in New Zealand, please write to the *Marketing Department, Penguin Books (NZ) Ltd, Private Bag, Takapuna, Auckland 9*

In India: For a complete list of books available from Penguin, please write to *Penguin Overseas Ltd, 706 Eros Apartments, 56 Nehru Place, New Delhi, 110019*

In Holland: For a complete list of books available from Penguin in Holland, please write to *Penguin Books Nederland B.V., Postbus 195, NL–1380AD Weesp, Netherlands*

In Germany: For a complete list of books available from Penguin, please write to *Penguin Books Ltd, Friedrichstrasse 10 – 12, D–6000 Frankfurt Main 1, Federal Republic of Germany*

In Spain: For a complete list of books available from Penguin in Spain, please write to *Longman Penguin España, Calle San Nicolas 15, E–28013 Madrid, Spain*

A CHOICE OF PENGUINS AND PELICANS

The Second World War (6 volumes) Winston S. Churchill

The definitive history of the cataclysm which swept the world for the second time in thirty years.

1917: The Russian Revolutions and the Origins of Present-Day Communism
Leonard Schapiro

A superb narrative history of one of the greatest episodes in modern history by one of our greatest historians.

Imperial Spain 1496–1716 J. H. Elliot

A brilliant modern study of the sudden rise of a barren and isolated country to be the greatest power on earth, and of its equally sudden decline. 'Outstandingly good' – *Daily Telegraph*

Joan of Arc: The Image of Female Heroism Marina Warner

'A profound book, about human history in general and the place of women in it' – Christopher Hill

Man and the Natural World: Changing Attitudes in England 1500–1800
Keith Thomas

'A delight to read and a pleasure to own' – Auberon Waugh in the *Sunday Telegraph*

The Making of the English Working Class E. P. Thompson

Probably the most imaginative – and the most famous – post-war work of English social history.

A CHOICE OF PENGUINS AND PELICANS

The French Revolution   Christopher Hibbert

'One of the best accounts of the Revolution that I know . . . Mr Hibbert is outstanding' – J. H. Plumb in the *Sunday Telegraph*

The Germans   Gordon A. Craig

An intimate study of a complex and fascinating nation by 'one of the ablest and most distinguished American historians of modern Germany' – Hugh Trevor-Roper

Ireland: A Positive Proposal   Kevin Boyle and Tom Hadden

A timely and realistic book on Northern Ireland which explains the historical context – and offers a practical and coherent set of proposals which could actually work.

A History of Venice   John Julius Norwich

'Lord Norwich has loved and understood Venice as well as any other Englishman has ever done' – Peter Levi in the *Sunday Times*

Montaillou: Cathars and Catholics in a French Village 1294–1324
Emmanuel Le Roy Ladurie

'A classic adventure in eavesdropping across time' – Michael Ratcliffe in *The Times*

Star Wars   E. P. Thompson and others

Is Star Wars a serious defence strategy or just a science fiction fantasy? This major book sets out all the arguments and makes an unanswerable case *against* Star Wars.

The Apartheid Handbook   Roger Omond

This book provides the essential hard information about how apartheid actually works from day to day and fills in the details behind the headlines.

The World Turned Upside Down   Christopher Hill

This classic study of radical ideas during the English Revolution 'will stand as a notable monument to . . . one of the finest historians of the present age' – *The Times Literary Supplement*

Islam in the World   Malise Ruthven

'His exposition of "the Qurenic world view" is the most convincing, and the most appealing, that I have read' – Edward Mortimer in *The Times*

The Knight, the Lady and the Priest   Georges Duby

'A very fine book' (Philippe Aries) that traces back to its medieval origin one of our most important institutions, marriage.

A Social History of England   New Edition   Asa Briggs

'A treasure house of scholarly knowledge . . . beautifully written and full of the author's love of his country, its people and its landscape' – John Keegan in the *Sunday Times*, Books of the Year

The Second World War   A J P Tavlor

A brilliant and detailed illustrated history, enlivened by all Professor Taylor's customary iconoclasm and wit.

FOR THE BEST IN PAPERBACKS, LOOK FOR THE 🐧

A CHOICE OF PENGUINS AND PELICANS

Adieux Simone de Beauvoir

This 'farewell to Sartre' by his life-long companion is a 'true labour of love' (the *Listener*) and 'an extraordinary achievement' (*New Statesman*).

British Society 1914–45 John Stevenson

A major contribution to the Pelican Social History of Britain, which 'will undoubtedly be the standard work for students of modern Britain for many years to come' – *The Times Educational Supplement*

The Pelican History of Greek Literature Peter Levi

A remarkable survey covering all the major writers from Homer to Plutarch, with brilliant translations by the author, one of the leading poets of today.

Art and Literature Sigmund Freud

Volume 14 of the Pelican Freud Library contains Freud's major essays on Leonardo, Michelangelo and Dostoevsky, plus shorter pieces on Shakespeare, the nature of creativity and much more.

A History of the Crusades Sir Steven Runciman

This three-volume history of the events which transferred world power to Western Europe – and founded Modern History – has been universally acclaimed as a masterpiece.

A Night to Remember Walter Lord

The classic account of the sinking of the *Titanic*. 'A stunning book, incomparably the best on its subject and one of the most exciting books of this or any year' – *The New York Times*

A CHOICE OF PENGUINS AND PELICANS

The Informed Heart   Bruno Bettelheim

Bettelheim draws on his experience in concentration camps to illuminate the dangers inherent in all mass societies in this profound and moving masterpiece.

God and the New Physics   Paul Davies

Can science, now come of age, offer a surer path to God than religion? This 'very interesting' (*New Scientist*) book suggests it can.

Modernism   Malcolm Bradbury and James McFarlane (eds.)

A brilliant collection of essays dealing with all aspects of literature and culture for the period 1890–1930 – from Apollinaire and Brecht to Yeats and Zola.

Rise to Globalism   Stephen E. Ambrose

A clear, up-to-date and well-researched history of American foreign policy since 1938, Volume 8 of the Pelican History of the United States.

The Waning of the Middle Ages   Johan Huizinga

A magnificent study of life, thought and art in 14th and 15th century France and the Netherlands, long established as a classic.

The Penguin Dictionary of Psychology   Arthur S. Reber

Over 17,000 terms from psychology, psychiatry and related fields are given clear, concise and modern definitions.

FOR THE BEST IN PAPERBACKS, LOOK FOR THE 🐧

A CHOICE OF PENGUINS AND PELICANS

The Literature of the United States Marcus Cunliffe

The fourth edition of a masterly one-volume survey, described by D. W. Brogan in the *Guardian* as 'a very good book indeed'.

The Sceptical Feminist Janet Radcliffe Richards

A rigorously argued but sympathetic consideration of feminist claims. 'A triumph' – *Sunday Times*

The Enlightenment Norman Hampson

A classic survey of the age of Diderot and Voltaire, Goethe and Hume, which forms part of the Pelican History of European Thought.

Defoe to the Victorians David Skilton

'Learned and stimulating' (*The Times Educational Supplement*). A fascinating survey of two centuries of the English novel.

Reformation to Industrial Revolution Christopher Hill

This 'formidable little book' (Peter Laslett in the *Guardian*) by one of our leading historians is Volume 2 of the Pelican Economic History of Britain.

The New Pelican Guide to English Literature Boris Ford (ed.)
Volume 8: The Present

This book brings a major series up to date with important essays on Ted Hughes and Nadine Gordimer, Philip Larkin and V. S. Naipaul, and all the other leading writers of today.